## Advance Praise for *Actively Unwoke*

"Karlyn Borysenko has been on the front lines of the fight against critical race theory from the very beginning. In *Actively Unwoke*, she brings together her experience as an organizational psychologist and as a fierce on-the-ground activist, exposing the myths underpinning woke politics and providing a pathway to defeating it. This book sets down another marker in the culture wars: wokeness is poison and, Borysenko argues, must be relegated to the dustbin of history."

**—Chris Rufo, the leader in the fight against critical race theory**

"Karlyn has been to the dark places that cancellation can take a person, and gained great wisdom from it. Her book will let you know what to expect when your workplace or social circle loses its collective mind, and will give you the mindset you need to keep your head and stand tall. It's a goldmine packed with stories of those who fought back, and strategies you can use to fight back yourself."

**—Paul Rossi, whistleblower exposing woke ideology in schools**

"In a market saturated with analytic critiques on Wokeness, Dr. Karlyn Borysenko offers something refreshingly original. *Actively Unwoke* is the intersection of *The Art of War*, Freud, and James Lindsay. It is a meditative battle tome for fighting Wokeness where it is most intrusive: our personal lives. I sorely wish this book had been available before my anti-Woke crusade in my school district. Dr. Borysenko's psychological expertise provides the structures and supports necessary to build the inner strength and harness the resiliency required to slay the Woke dragon unscathed. I highly recommend *Actively Unwoke* to all those that have had enough and are ready to fight but need a comprehensive and psychologically-integrative strategy to do so."

**—Frank McCormick, Chalkboard Heresy, whistleblower exposing critical race theory in schools**

"Karlyn Borysenko is a fearless warrior fighting a battle on two ideological fronts. She will challenge your worldview, partisanship notwithstanding. In an age where so many are trapped inside of their own political echo chambers, hers is a much-needed voice of reason and intellectual accountability."

**—Eric Matheny, cohost of *Bob & Eric Save America***

"Timely, relevant, insightful, lifesaving! In an *upside-down inside-out* world, Dr. Karlyn Borysenko has done a service to humanity and sensibility by writing this book. A must read…for these times and all times."

**—Howard Asher, psychotherapist and author of *A Loose Grip***

"In this honest and compelling book, knitting psychologist turned anti-woke superhero Karlyn Borysenko manages to do what so many have failed to do; she breaks down into plain, easy-to-understand language what 'woke' is. Highly recommended for anyone who has ever wondered what is all the fuss about Critical Race Theory and why it is so imperative to take action *now* to stop its ever-expanding encroachment into almost every area of our culture: government, schools, workplaces, sports, and religious institutions. If you value honesty, integrity, and freedom, then you need to read this book!"

**—Jodi Shaw, whistleblower exposing woke discriminatory practices at Smith College**

# ACTIVELY UNWOKE

## THE ULTIMATE GUIDE FOR FIGHTING BACK AGAINST THE WOKE INSANITY IN YOUR LIFE

Karlyn Borysenko

Published by Bombardier Books
An Imprint of Post Hill Press
ISBN: 978-1-63758-272-5
ISBN (eBook): 978-1-63758-273-2

Actively Unwoke:
The Ultimate Guide for Fighting Back Against the Woke Insanity in Your Life


Cover Design by Tiffani Shea

Post Hill Press
New York • Nashville
posthillpress.com

Published in the United States of America
1 2 3 4 5 6 7 8 9 10

*Dedicated to my husband, Victor.*
*Without you, I don't think I would have survived any of this.*

# Contents

# Introduction

## You Are NOT a Racist

The most important thing that you need to understand about the woke in this country is that, for their leaders, everything is about power. EVERYTHING. And the easiest way to gain power over another human being is to scare them into silence.

On the woke political left, they do this by calling everyone who disagrees with them a racist. That's the easiest way to gain power and control over another human being in our current reality.

Think about it: "Racist" is the very worst thing you can be called in our society. It is virtually irredeemable. Instantly, your friends and family look at you differently, wondering if it's really true. Your employer may reconsider if you deserve a job. You may lose your banking privileges, your credit card providers may cut you off, and you could be canceled, banned, or censored on the largest social media sites in the world—the places that have literally become the modern town square. They take your voice away, both figuratively and literally.

All of these outcomes, and more, have happened simply by someone on the left declaring that a person they wanted power over was a racist and, most of the time, no evidence of actual racism is required. In fact, if you deny your racism once you have been accused, people like Robin DiAngelo, author of the *New York Times* bestseller *White Fragility*, will tell you that your denial is PROOF of your racism. The more you deny the charge, the more proof they have of your obvious guilt.

This tactic by the left is nothing new. Sure, there was a sharp uptick in the accusations of racism under Donald Trump's presidency, but it was far from the first time the woke left played the race card.

Though some have pegged this phenomenon starting much earlier, it can minimally be traced to the 1970s with the publication of Saul Alinsky's *Rules for Radicals*. Coincidentally, that's also when white voters in the South were exiting the Democratic Party to join the GOP in disproportionately high rates after decades of historic support. What better way to rationalize the loss of those critical voters than to play the race card? After all, they're white. They're from the South. They MUST be racist. And the more this demographic supported the Republican Party, the more racist the party was portrayed by a woke left desperate to retain power.

Ronald Reagan was called a racist for championing welfare reform and for his war on drugs (though when Joe Biden joined the war on drugs and expanded the criminal penalties for convictions, the "D" next to his name was enough to help him avoid the "racism" charge).

George H. W. Bush was called a racist for the Willie Horton ad his campaign ran in an effort to depict him as the law-and-order candidate, while opponent Michael Dukakis was letting convicted murderers out for weekend furloughs. Willie Horton received one of those furloughs and used it to escape and commit more crimes. Bush was deemed racist for pointing that out.

George W. Bush had a plethora of racism charges made against him, including that he was racist for the administration's slow response to Hurricane Katrina, for wanting to invest more in border security, and for pushing immigration reform.

John McCain (a hero on the left today) got called a racist when he was running against Barack Obama. The *New York Times* accused him of "racially tinged attacks." Civil rights icon John Lewis charged that McCain was "sowing the seeds of hatred and division." *Teen Vogue* asserted that McCain was "patently Islamophobic." CNN anchor Don Lemon tweeted "the question is do you think the mccain [*sic*] campaign is creating a political environment that is inciting hate and hate speech?"

Even Mitt Romney, another current golden boy on the left since he voted to remove Donald Trump from office in his impeachment trial, was accused of racism once upon a time. And he was accused of it by none other than Joe Biden, who told a majority black audience that Romney wanted to "put y'all back in chains" at a campaign stop in Virginia during the 2012 presidential campaign. When Romney pushed back on the remark, the *New York Times* declared that denial was PROOF of his racism, paving the way for DiAngelo's work just a few years later.

And of course, Donald Trump was declared the most racist of them all, mostly for quotes that were taken completely out of context. The most infamous is the very fine people hoax, the moment Joe Biden credits with inspiring him to run for the presidency. What you've probably heard is that Trump called white supremacists and neo-Nazis in Charlottesville "very fine people." Put the quote in context, however, and you immediately discover that he also said the following:

> "I'm not talking about the neo-Nazis and the white nationalists. They should be condemned totally. You had many people in that group other than neo-Nazis and white nationalists. The press has treated them absolutely unfairly."

But the corporate media left that part out, played the first part of the statement on an endless loop, and spent the next four years declaring that Donald Trump had never condemned white supremacy.

So, congratulations. If you have been called a racist in your life by someone on the woke left or have ever been afraid of having the label hurled at you, you are in good company. Literally every major Republican politician and their supporters for the last forty years have been called racist. There is always a rationalization the left and their propaganda arm (the corporate "mainstream" media) can sell to their viewers. The charge, once levied, is inescapable until you bend the knee—notice that McCain and Romney both returned to the good graces of the left and the media when they began opposing Donald Trump.

Now, you might not be a Republican, and that's OK. I'm not one either! The point is to understand the game at play, one that uses language as one of its most powerful tactics. This was a game invented by people who are only interested in silencing their opponents so that power is easier to obtain and hold on to.

We need heroes who are willing to fight back despite the odds. Heroes who are willing to stand up and have their voices heard, even when it may come at a personal cost. Heroes who are willing to take on this fight, not because it is easy, but because it is hard.

In order to effectively defend against what the woke is doing to this country, you have to know emphatically that the label of "racist" does not apply to you or else you will be forever stunted and at their mercy.

*You are NOT a racist.*

Now listen, I can't guarantee that a rogue member of the KKK, ACTUAL neo-Nazi, or white identitarian didn't get their hands on a copy of this book, but the reality is that there is not as much racism in this country as the woke left would have you believe. Does it exist? Yes (and we'll talk about that later). But is 50 percent of the country racist purely because they didn't vote for a Democrat president? No.

If you believe that any one group of people is truly superior to all others based on nothing more than the color of their skin, you've got some soul searching to do (and, let's be honest, probably some therapy as well). Same goes for anyone who might believe that a white ethnostate is a good idea, or that the woke left is only out to elicit a white genocide. These are fearmongering tactics on the right that do not help us fight the larger cultural battle at play.

But if your only crime is believing that America is a pretty great place to live, that it is a land of opportunity, and that our liberties and freedoms are important to protect for everyone, then I need you to look in the mirror and repeat after me:

*You are NOT a racist.*

It is not racist to believe that freedom of speech should be absolute.

It is not racist to want to practice your religion or spirituality.

It is not racist to believe in small government.

It is not racist to disagree with a non-white person.

It is not racist to oppose universal healthcare.

It is not racist to believe that taxation is theft.

It is not racist to oppose the COVID lockdowns, mandatory vaccinations, or vaccine passports.

It is not racist to believe that individuals can achieve whatever they put their mind to, regardless of the color of their skin.

It is not racist to believe that America is the best, freest country in the history of the world.

It is not racist to believe children should be taught in schools how lucky they are to live here.

It is not racist to push back on any charge of racism levied against you purely because of who you support politically.

And denying that you are a racist is not proof of your racism, no matter what Robin DiAngelo, Ibram X. Kendi, or the *New York Times* wants to sell you.

*You are NOT a racist.*

These should be statements of obvious fact. But, sadly, things have gotten so out of control on the woke left that they have literally changed the dictionary definition of "racism" in order to accommodate their new standard.

After George Floyd's death and the anti-racist protests and riots that swept the nation, recent college graduate Kennedy Mitchum suggested to *Merriam-Webster* that they update their definition of "racism." And they bent the knee, revising their definition to include "the systemic oppression of a racial group to the social, economic, and political advantage of another." It is this definition that the woke left uses to define anyone who disagrees with their agenda as a racist.

We'll discuss more later about why the whole idea of systemic racism is nonsense. For now, here's all you need to know:

*You are NOT a racist.*

The woke left has been quietly and covertly fighting this battle for decades. Today, they control the most powerful forces in our country: the schools, the universities, the government, and the media. We have now reached a point where they literally begin teaching our children how to be little woke activists as early as elementary school and reinforce those lessons through middle school, high school, and college.

Once they're out of school, they get these ideas reinforced every single day by CNN, MSNBC, the *New York Times*, the *Washington Post*, and almost every other major media outlet in existence that calls all of their detractors, even the non-white ones, racist.

*You are NOT a racist.*

You won't even escape this ideology in the workplace. I'm an organizational psychologist by trade, someone who traveled the country doing trainings on how to be an effective manager and teaching mindfulness strategies in the workplace prior to the pandemic. After George Floyd's death, woke training took over my industry. It was near impossible to sell trainings that were not overly "anti-racist" in their nature, a code word for teaching people they are racist if they disagree.

It used to be that people assumed that kids would graduate from college and get forced into the real world when they got a real job. Now, these organizations coddle their young employees, even paying tens of thousands of dollars per day to bring woke trainers in to reinforce the ideology. If you think everyone is going crazy around you, you are not alone.

*You are NOT a racist.*

Critical Race Theory—the ideology of the woke that we will be focusing on in this book—isn't really about race. It's not about creating a more fair or equal or just society.

It is ONLY about power.

They utilize it because focusing on race is both the easiest way to keep people fighting each other AND the easiest way to keep people submissive to the mob. If they're focused on each other, that means they aren't looking at where the real enemy is—those who profit off of keeping the divisions going.

In fact, this ideology has created a lot of useful idiots who are just as toxic to the people they label as oppressed as it is for the oppressors, teaching them they will forever be defined by the color of their skin and that the world will always work against them.

Some argue that the woke ideology is anti-white. This is a terribly short-sighted view that fails to acknowledge that the ideology is anti-everyone. It *loves* white people who agree with it. It *hates* white people who disagree with it. This ideology teaches that black people are incapable of working hard, telling time, or getting a driver's license without the help of liberal white saviors to lift them up. Those ideas are incredibly racist, and they try to gaslight you into believing that you are a racist merely as projection of their own unmanaged baggage.

*You are NOT a racist.*

In order to become actively unwoke, you must get over any fear you have of being called a racist, knowing that the accusation itself says more about the person making it than it does about you. No matter what anyone says or what they try to convince you of, you have to believe with every fiber of your being that what they are saying is absolute bunk. Do not let them trick you! Stand your ground. Know that you're doing the right thing.

When you stop being afraid of being called a racist, you take their power away from them. When enough people take their power away, that's when we can start to fix the damage they have done.

*You are NOT a racist.*

Do you get it yet?

*You are NOT a racist.*

You're about to join the battle for our whole way of life, for the beacon of hope that the United States has been for the world for the last 250 years.

This fight isn't about Democrat or Republican. It's not about liberal values or conservative values.

It's about American values.

*Are you ready?*

OK, now we can get to work.

# PART 1

## Lay of the Land

# Welcome to the Resistance

In 2019, a guy named Zach Goldberg took to LexisNexis to do some research on how frequently the term racism showed up in the *New York Times* between 1980 and 2018. He found that between 1980 and 2014 things were pretty consistent with about three hundred to six hundred articles a year with the term racism mentioned in them. It peaked in the early 1990s before dipping back down to a low point by 2010.

Yay! If the *New York Times* isn't writing about racism, that *must* mean society is getting less racist!

But then something funny started to happen.

By 2015, the number of articles mentioning racism shot up to around eight hundred, the highest it had ever been since 1980.

One year later, it increased to fourteen hundred.

In 2017, it was over two thousand.

And by 2018, it was around twenty-four hundred.

What happened in this country to inspire the corporate media to more than quadruple their articles about racism in such a brief period? Was there a series of high-profile hate crimes? An epidemic of cross burnings? Was the Civil Rights Act of 1964 repealed?

No, none of the above. The answer is Occupy Wall Street happened.

For all the flaws of Occupy Wall Street (and there were many), it was a brief moment in time when a populist uprising of everyday people came together to focus their ire at the establishment elites who control the majority of the wealth and power in this country. It was one of those rare moments that we were all in agreement on who the actual enemy is.

This act of defiance could not go unpunished. To make sure it never happened again, the establishment pumped out enough propaganda to convince enough people that racism is just as alive and well in the United States as it was before the Civil Rights Movement.

And it worked! The same people who were occupying Zuccotti Park during Occupy turned their attention away from the establishment and to fighting the evil racists that had suddenly taken over the country, complete with Donald Trump being portrayed as their leader after he ascended to the presidency. It was all a farce, but it didn't matter. The elite shifted the battlefield, and thy name was *RACISM*.

Once they had refocused everyone's attention, they turned to milking it for all it was worth. The media, discovering they had accidentally stumbled onto a cash cow, continued this fearmongering, constantly reinforcing the idea that every good person out there is surrounded by racists on all sides. This kept the shares and clicks rolling in. Suddenly, *everything* in the United States became about race.

Here are just a few examples of things that have been declared racist by the media in the last few years, and I swear I'm not making any of these up:

- Math
- Traffic signals
- Soap
- Beer
- Dance
- Dr. Seuss
- Milk
- Trees
- Hockey
- Cycling
- Cereal
- Gandhi
- English
- Abraham Lincoln
- Swimming
- Classical music
- Owning a dog, and even dogs themselves

I'm sure my chihuahua (who is black, but that doesn't seem to matter) is filled with unconscious bias and thinking deeply racist thoughts as we speak. I can tell by the skeptical look on her face. And if she denies she's being racist by barking or demanding a belly rub, that's just proof of her dog fragility.

All of this worked so well that in his first major speech as president in 2021, Joe Biden named white supremacy as the most dangerous threat facing the United States.

That leads us to the first thing you need to understand about the woke movement that has infected our culture: It is not an accident. It is entirely by design.

It's not just silly college students regurgitating what they heard from their Marxist professors. It's not something the kids will just grow out of. It's not about the Black Lives Matter protests, building an equitable utopia, or any of the other things its adherents might say they are fighting for.

What's going on is bigger than any of us. This is a concerted effort by nefarious actors to gain and maintain power by hijacking the good intentions of millions of people who simply are not paying close enough attention to know they are being used. I do not believe the majority of the people buying into the woke ideology really understand what's going on—they are doing it because they've been brainwashed into believing that this is what is required to be a good person. We must keep this in mind as we are fighting them—it's just a few at the very top who understand what's going on.

The most important thing to understand is that it's not something that will just blow over and go away. It only takes a very small percent of the population—around 20 percent according to physicist Serge Galam—to shift the culture of any social system as long as that small percentage is highly vocal and inflexible.

The reality is this: The people who have the most power in any social system are the ones who are the most expressive—they are screaming from the rooftops what they think. They don't have to have the most brilliant idea. They just need to scream that idea the loudest.

The woke are very good at screaming. A very small, vocal minority of our society is being weaponized for the sake of cultural revolution, and it is not something that is going to stop until the majority wake up, speak up, and start fighting back. That's what we'll explore in this book—strategies you can use in your daily life to fight back the woke menace.

## It's OK to Be Overwhelmed

If that seems like a lot to process, it should. Everyone has a moment where they wake up and see for the first time. Mine was sitting in a car parked on the side of the road having so much cognitive dissonance that I had a pounding headache. That was my red pill moment.

If you picked up this book before taking the red pill (a concept based on the movie *The Matrix* to illustrate seeing reality as it truly is), this probably seems like a lot. We've all been there. The important thing is that you stay in it instead of running away from it. Do you want to see the world as it really is, or do you want to get inserted back into the Matrix where you can taste steak again?

Once you swallow the red pill, there's no going back. And you need to know that the reality we are facing right now is not a pretty one. The woke control every major institution in this county: the government, the corporate media, the universities, the public schools, and almost every major Fortune 100 company.

They are integrating their lessons in public, private, and charter schools across the country for students as young as four years old. Kids are learning to be good little anti-racists before they are learning how to read.

It's required coursework in every major university, including the elite military academies. If, by some chance, your kids escape it in primary and secondary school, they will 100 percent encounter the lessons the woke are teaching in college, where diversity of thought is a fantasy at best. According to research from the National Association of Scholars, over 90 percent of all faculty members consider themselves on the political left.

But surely, they'll learn once they graduate and enter the real world, right? Wrong. We used to think that the kids would wise up when they got their first professional job and had a boss to answer to. That's not the reality anymore. After George Floyd's death in 2020, the workplace went completely woke, which had corporations cowering to the social media mobs because they were more scared of mean tweets than they were of diminishing profit margins.

It really did change that quickly, at the snap of a finger. That's not to say that anti-racist training in the workplace didn't exist before that—it had been around for about a decade—but its sudden and deliberate prioritization ahead of all other forms of professional development was new and unprecedented.

And no matter where we go, we're surrounded.

- It's in the corporate media.
- It's in big tech.
- It's in Hollywood.
- It's even in the church.

There is not a single industry that this hasn't touched. And if it hasn't hit your workplace yet, consider yourself lucky, but do not consider yourself safe. It will come at some point, and you don't want to wait until it does to deal with this impending reality.

## There's No One Coming to Save You

This is a book about fighting back. It's about a ragtag group of underdogs coming together to save the country, and we want you to be on our team. It doesn't matter where you are in life, your job, your race, your gender, where you live, or any other factor that the woke will tell you makes you either part of an oppressed group or the oppressor themselves. The unwoke army is truly inclusive because we have one goal and one goal only: the preservation of the values and liberties the country was founded on almost 250 years ago.

The woke would have you believe that the fight taking place is a matter of political affiliation—Democrat versus Republican, left versus right, the righteous versus the insurgents.

But that's just not true. Being unwoke is not about belonging to a specific political party. Basic liberties like freedom of speech, freedom of assembly, and freedom of religion are not conservative values—these are American values. We don't need to agree on every political issue and nuance in order to come together and agree that we do want to preserve the Union.

In order to win, we have to come together despite our differences and contribute in the ways that each of us are able. This book will give you examples of a variety of ways people have fought back to inspire you. But you shouldn't limit yourself just to the tactics here—this is a time for creativity. If you have ideas about how to fight this menace, it is your responsibility to champion them.

Most importantly, I need you to resist the urge to run away and pretend the problem doesn't exist, because that's exactly what has put us into this position to begin with. We are at a critical inflection point in American history in which our collective actions in addressing this problem will determine the future of this country. If you ever wondered what you would have done during the Civil Rights Movement, or even in Germany in the 1930s, what you are doing right now is the answer to that question. If we do not beat this enemy back now, we may not have the chance to again.

If you're reticent, I get it. Believe me when I tell you that stepping up to fight the woke was not a part of my life plan.

I was a Democrat for twenty years, from the time I was eighteen years old, and never had any intention of leaving the party. I grew up in Vermont, the land of hippie liberals, Ben & Jerry's, and Bernie Sanders. I'd voted for Bernie in every election that I was able to up until 2020, protested George W. Bush's wars in college, breathed a sigh of relief with Obama's win in 2008 (and voted for him again in 2012), and even voted for Hillary in 2016. When I woke up the day after the 2016 election to find that Donald Trump had pulled off the upset of the century, I cried. Yes, I was one of those people.

Then something funny happened: social justice took over my knitting community.

Yes, I said knitting. The thing with the yarn and the needles that results in a misshapen sweater that your grandmother gives you for Christmas after she's been working on it for a full year leading up to the occasion.

I know when people think of knitting, that's exactly what they think of—old ladies sitting around, drinking tea, and gossiping with their knitting group. However, there are a lot of younger knitters out there creating beautiful, unorthodox designs...and many are deeply progressive. Where do you think all those pink pussy hats came from? The knitters, of course!

I taught myself how to knit when I was in my twenties, but didn't get seriously into knitting until I was in my mid-thirties after I discovered beautiful hand-dyed yarn that was about a thousand times better than the awful synthetic yarn you'd get at a store like Michaels or Hobby Lobby. From there I was hooked. I spent all my spare time knitting, talking about knitting, looking at pictures of knitting, and so on.

When you're spending a lot of money on beautiful yarn, and it takes weeks or months to make a single project from it, there was no better place to show off your work than Instagram. That's where I discovered the newest patterns and explored all of the unique creative things people did with them. It was fun. Most importantly, it was an escape—a place to just look at pretty things and leave the cares of the world behind.

And then social justice took over my knitting community.

You wouldn't think a movement called "social justice" would be like a dark plague that would ruin everything it touches, but this is exactly what happened. I've since learned that the knitting wars were underway long before I was ever aware of them, like water being brought to a slow boil. At the time, it seemed like one day out of nowhere, a roving gang of social justice warriors just showed up and started wreaking havoc on the knitting world.

Here are just a few of the things they did:

- They attacked a maker of very fancy knitting bags named Karen Templer for writing a blog post expressing excitement over an upcoming trip to India and forced her to write a long apology pointing out everything that was wrong with the initial post.
- They attacked yarn-dyer Maria Tusken for daring to defend Templer. She refused to bend the knee to their demands and, in return, they attempted to destroy her business.
- They attacked a gay man who goes by Sockmatician for posting a poem asking for kindness, claiming he was tone policing. He was bullied and mobbed so badly that he had a nervous breakdown and ended up in the hospital on suicide watch.
- And they attacked pattern designer Caitlin Hunter for saying nothing at all and not taking a side, because silence is considered both violence and complicity.

These are just a few of the attacks that took place. I watched this happening, not understanding why everyone in the knitting world suddenly seemed to be issuing compelled statements denouncing people for infractions that seemed so minor they weren't even worthy of an ounce of attention. None of the people who were attacked had done anything wrong, and yet there was still an angry mob of people with virtual torches and pitchforks hellbent on destroying their lives.

If you've never experienced an online mobbing, either as an onlooker, a participant, or as the target, it's hard to explain the sheer velocity of hundreds of people coming at you with more hate and vitriol than you've ever experienced in your life in unrelenting attacks. Defending yourself is fruitless because any attempt to defend yourself is taken as nothing more than proof of your obvious guilt. What these social justice mobs do is the very definition of bullying.

I studied bullying in the workplace for over a decade and had done my doctoral dissertation about how young professionals cope with being a target of workplace bullying. So, I know bullying when I see it. This wasn't fair. It wasn't justice. It wouldn't lead to more "equitable" outcomes. It was just plain bullying. I watched this play out over the course of months, afraid of what would happen to me if I spoke up.

On October 15, 2019, I mustered up the courage to finally get in the game and say something. I figured the people who were most susceptiable to being attacked were those who relied on knitting for their income from things like owning a yarn store, working as a pattern designer, and the like. I didn't do any of those things (I just wanted to knit!), so I thought I could speak up without much fear of consequences.

I made a post to my Instagram that read as follows:

> "BULLYING is when someone is targeted for isolation, humiliation, and aggression when they don't have the ability to defend themselves."

It was an abbreviated definition for sure, but one only has so much room in a small square image. I added the post to my feed and waited. And, sure enough, the woke mob started to descend—how DARE I question their methods, and I obviously just needed to be educated!

But guess what: my calculation that there was nothing they could really do to hurt me was correct. They screamed and shouted and carried on and sent me horrible messages…but at the end of the day, I survived. More importantly, I learned that the woke mob only has the power that we allow them to have over us. In *Rules for Radicals*, Saul Alinsky wrote that fear of "the thing" is often greater than the thing itself. I had overcome my fear of "the thing" to speak up, and that was the hardest part. Once I had spoken up, I felt this new life surge through me. It was OK to stand up for what I believed in. I could make it through in one piece!

I considered the post itself a win, regardless of the reaction to it. Even more than that, it was exhilarating! It felt amazing to speak up and say what I knew was true no matter what the mob thought about it. I've been fighting back ever since. I've had ups and downs, some of which we'll talk about in this book. I've received tens of millions of views on my work and have impacted real change…and I've experienced being canceled, ostracized, and shunned.

Here's what I want you to know: No matter the hardships that come with being in the game, it is absolutely worth it. I wouldn't change a thing. This is a fight worth having.

Every single person reading this will have different ways to contribute in this fight, and there is no contribution that is more or less important than others. You may be able to fight the battle in the open, or you may need to focus on private conversations with friends and family—both types of efforts are necessary. Don't let fear of the "how" to fight back deter you from making the commitment to get in the game.

Our actions in this moment must not be guided by what is convenient but by what is necessary.

We are the resistance.

We are the counterculture.

And we need as many people as possible to join the fight in any way that they can.

Pretending it's not happening is no longer an option.

It's time to get in the game.

# Decoding the Woke

I've already told you the story about my foray into the knitting wars, but another funny thing happened to me around the same time that provoked me to jump into the fight against the woke.

You see, I worked in higher education for about ten years, both at different colleges and universities and at consulting companies that served them. That meant a good bit of my social circle was made up of higher education professionals from around the county. In fact, my closest friends all worked in higher ed and were deeply connected to the institutions that spawned the woke threat. We even had a name for our group—The Kittens. We were so close that I may or may not have a kitten emoji tattoo.

One day, my friends seemed to change their demeanor completely, demanding out of nowhere that I "shut up and listen to black people," eliminate all gendered language from my vocabulary, and join a *White Fragility* book club. I had known these women for years. I had traveled around the country with them, gotten ink with them, even had dinner with one at her grandmother's house. From my perspective, it was as if they had changed into pod people overnight, à la *Invasion of the Body Snatchers*. I didn't recognize these people anymore, and they seemed to be shells of themselves.

But they were my friends, and I wanted to give them the benefit of the doubt. So, I tried to take it seriously and attempted to have a reasonable conversation about why I didn't think this was a very good way to fix racism. I found the "shut up" demand particularly problematic. As a psychologist who works with groups, I understand that you don't create an environment of empathy or compassion when you're telling one group of people to "shut up"—the only way to create understanding is through discussions and dialogue. It was deeply confusing to me that my friends were turning into a mob demanding that those around them shut up and conform. In the time I had known some of these people, the words "shut up" had never left their mouths without being facetious, at least not directed at me, and certainly not as a condition for being considered a good person.

When I brought these concerns up, I was immediately rebuffed. "No," they declared, "the only way for a white person to be a good ally is to shut up and listen to the experiences of black people." If I did anything less than that, I was obviously a racist that wasn't interested in working through my own fragility. None of it made any sense to me. Why was I suddenly a racist?! It seemed like we had all been perfectly normal people just a week ago!

I loved my friends. And because of that, I continued to try to compromise even though I didn't believe in the "shut up" strategy at all. I wanted to keep an open mind. After all, maybe they understood something I didn't! So, I connected with a black anti-racist trainer in the knitting community who was exploring these issues. She posted materials online to help white people become good anti-racist allies, so I started watching to see what she had to say. And lo and behold, one of her videos was about how white people needed to stop telling other white people to shut up and listen to black people!

"Ah ha!" I thought, as I fist pumped in the air. "If this is coming from a black anti-racist trainer, it should convince them that telling people to shut up won't work!"

Au contraire. When I reported back to my friends that I had done what they had asked—that I had shut up and listened to black people, and the person I listened to said it wasn't a good idea to tell people to shut up just like I originally said—I was told I was just tokenizing that particular black anti-racist trainer and so I was still wrong. Apparently, I had not shut up and listened to the *right* black people.

At this point that I realized that there was no winning. No matter what I did, if I didn't bend the knee to this groupthink they had all become infected by, I would always be wrong. Every single time they'd find an excuse to rationalize it, even if that excuse completely contradicted something they had told me a day or two prior. It was a heartbreaking realization that the people I knew and loved just weren't there anymore. Imagine everyone you've told your secrets to for the last several years just suddenly vanished and were replaced with something that looked like them but wasn't them at all.

They had become pod people. Just because they looked like normal people doesn't mean they acted like normal people. They had been assimilated into a hive mind of sorts. When you look at this happening long enough, you start to see a pattern to the language and tactics of the ideology.

I watch a lot of woke trainings to understand what they're doing and how they're doing it. Sometimes, I can predict exactly what woke trainers or facilitators will say, because they all use the same language and script in every interaction, even if they work for different organizations and have never met each other in real life. Even when they are trying to outmaneuver you by changing definitions to suit their purposes or seeming to operate without any sort of consistency in how they apply their values, there is still a pattern in their behavior.

For the remainder of this chapter, I'll decode the elements of the woke ideology to help you start to see those patterns emerge in your own life.

## To Fight the Woke, You Must Understand Them

The goal of the woke mindset is to constantly reinforce the woke mindset, nothing more. Anything that disrupts this goal must be discredited and eliminated from their experience, no matter what. Logic and reason don't matter in the Orwellian world of the woke—if you try to fight them using logic and reason, you will fail because it is simply not something they value. All that matters is protecting the ideology at all costs.

This all makes it very hard for average, everyday people who are not part of this hive mind to understand what is going on or even to identify that something is wrong. If it seems as though they are speaking a completely different language, it's because they probably are. So, if you find yourself confused by the language they're using and the demands they are making, fear not! You are not alone. This chapter will help you dissect what's really going on.

There are wonderful books out there to help you understand the woke ideology. *Cynical Theories* by James Lindsay and Helen Pluckrose will take you on a guided tour through the academic literature. *The Madness of Crowds* by Douglas Murray will illustrate how it's showing up in pop culture. *The Coddling of the American Mind* by Greg Lukianoff and Jonathan Haidt will tell you about its impact on children.

However, what I want to do here is some basic decoding to provide practical knowledge that average people (the ones who have jobs and kids and sometimes just want to be able to relax and watch the game on the weekends) can use to understand and interact with the woke in their lives. I'm not only going to tell you what the woke are saying—I'm also going to tell you how to read between the lines and interpret it.

If you're looking for an intellectual discussion of this mindset, I'm sorry to say that I'm not your girl. There are any number of intellectuals who will intellectualize for hours on the internet about the woke. The problem is that all that intellectualizing very rarely wins any real victories against them. Sometimes those with the most academic knowledge are the ones who are the least willing to do anything with that knowledge.

That's not what we're doing here. Being actively unwoke is not about having discussions with people who agree with you to show off how smart you are. We don't just *talk* about things. We *do* things.

But in order to gain very real wins, you must understand the rules of the game we're playing. What we're going for here is down and dirty, my brain dump of the knowledge

I've acquired from being in this fight every day for the past few years.

## What It Means to Be "Woke"

The word "woke," as it's used today, was added to *Merriam-Webster* in 2017, which defined it as "aware of and actively attentive to important facts and issues (especially issues of racial and social justice)."

More colloquially, it means someone who is awake to the horrors of injustice in the world—a bit ironic since "woke" is the past tense of "awake."

How we will use it in the context of this book is far more simple: To be woke is to be a little authoritarian. It is to insist that everyone in the world live by your standards and to promise retribution in the form of social rejection and mob attack if they do not. They see things that aren't there, maintain a snobbish air of superiority over everyone who disagrees with them, and will downright attempt to silence anyone who gets in their way. Their ideology destroys everything it touches given enough time.

Anyone of any political ideology can be woke. Our primary focus in this book is on the woke political left, because they currently represent the greatest threat to our country and our values. Unless it's specified otherwise, you can assume that any mention of "woke" generally refers to the political left.

However, make no mistake: woke exists on the political right, too, mostly as their response to what the left has been driving towards for decades. We'll touch on woke on the right briefly as a warning for everyone who thinks this is only coming from one side. All wokism is bad and must be condemned; it doesn't matter which team you're on.

When it comes to identifying the woke in the real world, practically speaking, you're going to find a person who covets political correctness, has a rigid, inflexible view of the world, and places race at the forefront of every issue and discussion, even if the discussion isn't substantively about the topic. That's because the woke are well versed in the tenants of Critical Race Theory (CRT).

If you don't know what that is, don't worry. This chapter will give you the CliffsNotes version of everything you need to know about the vocabulary the woke are using so you can easily pick out the language when it's brought up in conversation. The woke use language as one of their greatest weapons because they manipulate it to confuse everyone. What I've tried to do is bring it down to absolute brass tacks—the essential elements that you need to know in order to identify and fight this ideology.

The italicized words are key words that you will hear coming up repeatedly in your interactions with the woke. You'll want to jot them down in your mental Rolodex to be prepared for when they come up.

Buckle up as we enter a world where down is up, left is right, racism is anti-racist, war is peace, and freedom is slavery.

## Racism Everywhere, but Not a Drop to Drink!

In his iconic speech, Martin Luther King Jr. said, "I have a dream that my four little children will one day live in a nation where they will not be judged by the color of their skin but by the content of their character."

The woke left want the opposite of what King envisioned: they believe the color of one's skin is the only thing that matters, with no regard to the content of their character.

This is the easiest way to understand *Critical Race Theory*. CRT is a fringe ideology with early roots in the Marxist Frankfurt School before manifesting in academia in the 1970s. It has progressively worked its way into every major part of our world. If you are living in the United States today, you have encountered CRT whether you know it or not.

The basic premise is this: Racism exists everywhere—in every person, every interaction, every organization, and every institution—and the goal of the critical theorist is to explore how (not if) racism occurred in each instance. Racism is always assumed to have occurred, and white people (the ones who built the system) are assumed to be racist from birth. In *White Fragility* (on page 51 to be exact), Robin DiAngelo writes, "Indeed, the forces of racism were shaping me even before I took my first breath."

Yes, the white woman who spawned a thousand book clubs after George Floyd's death wrote that she had been a racist since the womb. She also happily confesses she is a racist at any of the high-priced keynotes she is hired to give.

The assumption that racism exists everywhere is the basis of *systemic racism*—the idea that racism is embedded in every system in society. The underlying premise is that our society was built by white people (usually men), and their whiteness would dictate that they only build systems that would support other white people. And then additional systems were built on top of those systems, and more systems were built upon those. Before you know it, VOILA! Systemic racism: an entire system set up for the sole benefit of one group based on the premise that white people only care about helping and supporting other white people.

This is how they've been able to change the definition of *racism* and *white supremacy*. Racism isn't just about a person believing that white people are better than black people. Instead, they've changed the definition to anyone who supports the current structures and systems in place, including capitalism, which they fault for all of our racial disparities. If only we tore down our current system and replaced it with something more resembling socialism! Then everything would be OK, and racism would be solved!

So you see, even though Critical Race Theory has "race" in the title, it's not about race at all. It's about bringing down a system (capitalism) that they claim upholds racism and white supremacy.

The woke view everything in terms of a collective unit, rather than as the individual parts that make up that unit. Their ideology has Marxist roots, which means that it is socialist in nature. Even the founders of Black Lives Matter admitted to being trained Marxists in videos that went viral on the internet in 2020.

I was a Democrat for twenty years before leaving the party in early 2020 when I came to the realization that they had abandoned the values of individual liberty and freedom that I had joined the party for. I bring this up because when I was a Democrat, and even still today, it drives me crazy when I hear conservatives and Republicans ranting about a socialist/communist agenda in relation to everything the political left wants to do. It's a default excuse they use to oppose something when they're too lazy to come up with a real argument or an alternative solution.

*However*, in this case they're actually not wrong.

I know that, for some of you, the threat of socialism/communism might seem silly or cheesy but in this case it's real, and you'll understand why as this chapter unfolds. For right now what you need to know is that wherever you sit on the political spectrum—left, right, center, or off in the land of the politically homeless—this is not one of those times where you should dismiss the idea of a socialist ideology attempting to corrupt our systems. That's literally happening in precisely the way Soviet defector Yuri Bezmenov told us it would in the 1980s. (Look up those videos on YouTube, if they haven't censored them yet.)

It makes sense, then, that the ideology would shift the definition of racism from an individual issue to a collective issue, because the collective is what they are interested in. They do not perceive white people as individuals with a diverse array of life experiences—they are viewed as a collective group who are all proud owners of *white privilege*. Their background, upbringing, and socioeconomic status do not matter—you could grow up in a mansion in Beverly Hills or a shack with no running water in Appalachia, and if you're white, you're still considered privileged.

The idea of white privilege comes from an essay titled "White Privilege: Unpacking the Invisible Knapsack" by one of the original anti-racists, Peggy McIntosh. I know it will shock you to learn that she's a feminist who was working for Wellesley College when this essay was written.

Even so, the essay is anything but academic. What Peggy essentially wrote was a list of assumptions and observations about all the benefits she (as a well-to-do white lady) had over someone who was black in America. The essay contained exactly zero academic citations or empirical evidence—it blossomed from Peggy's head and into the hearts and minds of social justice activists everywhere. It includes statements like, "If I want to, I can be pretty sure of finding a publisher for this piece on white privilege," and, "I am never asked to speak for all the people of my racial group."

Although this essay is still held up today, thirty years later, as proof of systemic racism, one cannot help but laugh when applying some of the statements to our current conditions. Of course, a non-white author will be able to find a publisher for a book about white privilege today (Ibram X. Kendi, anyone?), and white people are blamed for the sins of other white people who died before they were born all the time.

If we updated the essay to current times, we might see something like the chart titled "Aspects & Assumptions of Whiteness and White Culture in the United States," which appeared in the National Museum of African American History and Culture in the summer of 2020. It defined whiteness as, among other things, having an emphasis on objective thinking, rugged individualism, being on time, planning for the future, and working hard.

(A logical person might question why the woke don't believe non-white people can work hard. In fact, some might argue that idea sounds a little racist.)

It's not just white people that the woke view as a collective—all people are judged for their race. However, if the group is non-white, they are simply assumed to be *oppressed* or *marginalized*, rather than power-hungry oppressors. The woke do not see human beings as individuals but rather as a collection of "bodies" who all share a common skin color. You'll frequently hear the woke use the term *black and brown bodies* to indicate that they see people based on how they appear outside, not who they are inside.

All of this reflects a concerted effort to shift language to the collective, because you can't implement a little socialism utopia without focusing on the collective rather than focusing on individual merit, hard work, and accomplishment.

But this shift in the definition of racism had to happen for a practical reason too: the woke just got too ridiculous in their accusations of racism, and it was just starting to look silly.

After years of cancel culture, with half of the country being accused of racism and white supremacy purely based on which political party they vote for, it just starts to look silly to assert that everyone is a racist if you don't change the definition of the word to something more generalizable. One of the easiest ways to begin to red pill people is simply to ask how half the country (or more!) could possibly be racist. It was a crack in the argument that had to be filled in order for adherents to continue to suspend disbelief in service to the ideology.

In response, the woke had to employ one of their many strategies to fend off criticism: *they had to shift the target.*

This is a strategy you must anticipate when you're fighting the woke. Remember how we've already established they don't care for logic and reason? Well, when the woke's arguments start to get shot down, they will typically just change the argument entirely, without any acknowledgement of losing the previous argument on logical grounds. After all, if they never admit they lost the fight, did it really happen?

What this does is it creates an unwinnable debate with a target that is running in circles all over the playing field. Every time you fire an arrow, the target simply steps to one side to avoid getting hit without acknowledging that it moved.

Let me show you how this works in the real world: New Hampshire was the first state to introduce legislation on a state level to address the problem of CRT (though, sadly, we were not the first state to pass such legislation because our Republican Governor Chris Sununu worked with Democrats to support CRT in schools, but I digress). I worked with the bill's sponsor, State Representative Keith Ammon, to help fight for the legislation and had a front row seat to the shenanigans at play.

When the bill was introduced, the first argument our woke opponents made is that it was racist, their go-to argument. However, since one of the first lines in the bill was a prohibition on teaching that one race was superior to another, this charge didn't stick. It was right there in black and white—you can't make assumptions based on someone's race. Therefore, how could the bill be racist?

The next argument they made was the bill was "transphobic." Since the bill didn't mention trans people at all, this argument also failed. It was a bizarre argument to make, but you'll understand why they did it when you understand that the woke believe trans people are oppressed beyond all other people. We'll explore more when we discuss the oppression hierarchy.

Next, they tried to say the bill was anti-free speech. This was the argument that tricked our idiot governor, who failed to read the brief provided to him by the former chief justice of the New Hampshire Supreme Court explaining that government employees do not have free speech protections when they are acting as agents of the state.

Later on in the process, they also moved into a late-blooming fourth shift of the target, just for fun: they declared the proponents of the bill didn't even know what Critical Race Theory was, even though the bill had very clear definitions included for what was and was not permissible!

They use this strategy all the time when they are losing the argument. I anticipate it will not be long before they attempt to change the Critical Race Theory name because of the mounting public outrage against it. They won't give up on their strategy—they'll just start calling it something else entirely and pretend that they don't understand why we might think they are doing anything nefarious!

It is all a means to an end, and they will say and do anything to achieve their goals almost without conscience.

## It's the System, Stupid

White adherents of the woke ideology are told it's not good enough to not be individually racist. Instead, their job as a white *ally* is to be *actively anti-racist.*

According to the woke, you are either a racist or you are an anti-racist. It is black and white—no compromise. You are either with them, or you are against them. And the allies who consider themselves to be anti-racists will constantly be on the lookout to call people out on their racist acts, even if it's only racist in the most ridiculous and distorted ways. This can lead to individuals calling each other out for "racist" acts for almost anything.

For example, did you forget to CC a work colleague who happens to be a person of color on an email? That's a *microaggression*, or a small act that indicates an *unconscious prejudice or bias* against the marginalized group in question. It would be completely fine if you had forgotten to CC a white colleague;

that's an innocent mistake! But apply the same rule to a colleague of color, and you obviously forgot because you're a racist.

Even worse, did you make a joke about nicknaming COVID "Kung Flu"? That was my personal favorite nickname for the virus. And I'm sorry, but it's hilarious. If you didn't have the song "Kung Fu Fighting" stuck in your head (but making it "Kung *Flu* Fighting" instead) during the very first "fifteen days to slow the spread" lockdown, I question your sense of humor and humanity. And I know many Asians who agree with me. But regardless...yeah, you're definitely racist for that.

However, being anti-racist isn't just about calling out small instances of racism—it's more nefarious than that. Remember, the woke view everything as a collective. That means that it's not good enough to call out individual acts of racism—good allies are supposed to focus on *systemic or institutional racism* ingrained in our system.

We've already explored why they had to move from the individual to the collective. Now, let's look at what those ideas look like in practice.

Ibram X. Kendi, author of *How To Be An Antiracist*, defines anti-racism as supporting and instituting policies that level out all racial disparities in regard to socioeconomic outcomes. Racism, then, is defined as supporting any policy or idea that results in racial inequity.

Kendi also famously quipped:

> The only remedy to racist discrimination is antiracist discrimination. The only remedy to past discrimination is present discrimination. The only remedy to present discrimination is future discrimination.

Yes, he is literally arguing that the solution for racism is racism.

And here we land on the idea of *equality versus equity*. If you thought the woke were just fighting for equal rights, think again. They are fighting for equal outcomes.

You know who else likes equal outcomes? Socialists.

The argument goes like this: Different racial groups have different outcomes in life. White people tend to make more money than black people. Asian people tend to get into better colleges than black people. Because the system seems to advantage some groups more than others, the only answer is to change the system to eliminate any and all racial disparities.

Leveling out racial disparities in regard to socioeconomic outcomes sounds like a nice idea, doesn't it? They'll tell you they just want to build a fair society where everyone has a fair shot. After all, that's what social justice is!

But the devil is in the details of how they want to do it.

Equality suggests that every single person, regardless of their race, gender, sexual orientation, gender identity, disability status, and the like, should have access to the same *opportunities* for success. No one should be denied a job purely because of their skin color or their gender. We can all agree on that.

Equity suggests that each person is guaranteed an equal outcome, and that some people might need to be propped up with additional help or resources beyond what the average person receives to get there. They believe in equal outcomes *regardless* of how an individual achieves along a variety of factors that can lead to individual success, including hard work, consistency, quality, commitment, communication, interpersonal skills, and so on.

Let's look at it another way:

- Equality guarantees an opportunity to succeed. Then you have to show up and put in the effort.
- Equity guarantees a successful outcome *regardless* of effort.

I once watched an eighth grade class, recorded by a fourteen-year-old student, in which the teacher used the following analogy: Say you have two hungry students, and you give them each a Big Mac. For one of those students, a single Big Mac was enough to fill them up. But the other student was left hungry after a single burger. The teacher asked if that was fair—is it fair that the second student only got one burger when they required two burgers to satiate their hunger? Equity of cheeseburgers, the teacher argued, was the only fair outcome. And the students, being fourteen-year-olds, agreed.

This teacher might agree with the saying, "From each according to his ability, to each according to his need," a slogan popularized by Karl Marx in his 1875 *Critique of the Gotha Program.*

This is how they are introducing the idea of equity to your children—that the only fair outcome is when they have everything they desire handed to them on a silver platter without having to work hard to come up with the additional few bucks in order to buy that second cheeseburger.

Where does the idea of equity lead?

Kurt Vonnegut wrote a short story called "Harrison Bergeron" about an equitable society in which everyone was guaranteed the same outcome. In that world, everyone was leveled out to mediocre levels. If you were too smart, you wore a headset that constantly made a buzzing sound to dumb you down to average. If you were too quick, you were made to wear weights to slow you down. They put purposeful handicaps on the most gifted members of society in order to balance out their privilege. It reminds me of this quote from Margaret Atwood in *The Handmaid's Tale*: "Better never means better for everyone.... It always means worse, for some."

A society grounded to the idea of equity is not equal, fair, or just to everyone. A constant state of mediocrity doesn't provide space for some people to be more successful than others without accusations of racism and injustice. It doesn't allow anyone to step into their greatness, because if you step into your greatness that means you set yourself apart from the average joe. Reality simply doesn't work like that unless we socially engineer it to be so. Human beings will always naturally have different wants, needs, desires, drives, and motivations that will lead them down different paths in life.

The woke will try to convince you that you are a racist if you believe that equality (equal access to opportunities) is better that equity (equal outcomes). They will tell you that you are supporting *colorblindness*, which is considered racist because they willfully misinterpret it as denying that people can have different experiences depending on race. When most people say colorblind, they just mean that you don't treat people differently because of their race. This should be perceived as a virtue, but doing so would undermine the entire woke ideology. They refuse to factor in that hard work is an individual trait, not one that you can assign to a collective group.

## Some Oppressed People Are More Oppressed Than Others

Given the Marxist underpinnings of the entire woke ideology, it should come as no surprise that they view the world as a constant *struggle for power*. Once you understand that everything the woke do is about gaining more and more power so that they can destabilize our system to build their socialist utopia, you will see their actions in a new light.

The woke consider white people holders of the ultimate power: a society where everything is built to benefit them exclusively, a foundation made possible because of all the racist white people who came before them and built the system in their image.

That means that everyone who is not white experiences oppression that gives them less power than white people. But not all oppression is created equal! The level of oppression one experiences is dependent, mostly, on the darkness of their skin.

Enter the oppression hierarchy, a somewhat rigid, unofficial hierarchy that tells you which groups score the most points on the victimhood scale. In its default state, the hierarchy generally looks like this, with the most oppressed people at the top:

- Black
- Native Americans
- Latino/Hispanic
- Asians
- Jews
- White

Those who are biracial or multiracial would fit in with the category that most closely resembles their skin color. If their skin is too light, they may be told that they are too *white-passing* to be considered oppressed. As an aside, I've personally witnessed anti-racist trainings for teachers in which the trainers instructed the teachers to urge their biracial students to identify with the non-white parent because the white parent is the oppressor.

## Earn Extra Oppression Points with Intersectionality

Although the woke place the most importance on race, that doesn't mean that it's the only way you can earn oppression points. Welcome to the wonderful world of *intersectionality*, where the woke gain points for a myriad of other characteristics that are (mostly) out of any person's control.

Coined by Kimberlé Crenshaw in 1989 (the same year that knapsack essay was written), intersectionality is essentially the idea that there are lots of different ways to be oppressed in the United States, and the more marginalized characteristics a person has, the more oppressed they can be.

For instance, here are some different categories of oppression people might experience:

| Characteristic | **Most oppressed** | **Somewhat oppressed** | **Least oppressed** |
|---|---|---|---|
| Gender | Trans men, trans women, or nonbinary | Cisgendered* women | Cisgendered* men |
| **To be cis is to identify with the gender assigned at birth. It's the opposite of trans.* | | | |

<table>
<tr><th>Characteristic</th><th>Most oppressed</th><th>Somewhat oppressed</th><th>Least oppressed</th></tr>
<tr><td>Sexuality</td><td>Pansexual, asexual*</td><td>Gay men and lesbians, and bisexuals to a lesser extent.</td><td>Heterosexuals</td></tr>
<tr><td colspan="4">*To be pansexual is to be attracted to people regardless of their sex or gender identity. To be asexual is to not be interested in sexual activity.</td></tr>
<tr><td>Socioeconomic status</td><td>Poor</td><td>Middle class</td><td>Wealthy</td></tr>
<tr><td>Disability status</td><td>Significantly disabled</td><td>Some disability</td><td>Able-bodied</td></tr>
<tr><td>Religion</td><td>Muslim</td><td>Jewish</td><td>Christian</td></tr>
<tr><td>Education</td><td>School drop out</td><td>High school graduate</td><td>College educated</td></tr>
<tr><td>Mental health and well-being</td><td>Severely traumatized</td><td>Depression, anxiety, ADD/ ADHD</td><td>Healthy</td></tr>
</table>

Intersectionality means that we can begin to have combinations of categories, along with racial categories, to create more opportunities for oppression!

For example, if a person is black and a trans woman, that is about the highest level of oppression points you can score because it combines two of the woke's favorite categories. Trans people are considered among the most oppressed of any oppression category because their numbers are so few and due to the more difficult nature of their experience compared with a person who is not born trans.

If you are white but you are also a woman who has to use a wheelchair in your daily life, you would gain oppression points because of your intersecting identities. You'd gain additional points if you struggled with depression or had experienced more severe trauma. You would never gain enough oppression points to match an able-bodied black person, however, because no matter how bad you've got it, you still have white privilege on your side.

If you grow up white and poor, you are considered to be less oppressed than your black poor neighbor who grew up right next door, even if all other circumstances are created equal. Heck, even if your black neighbor had more money than you because his father was the manager in the company your dad worked at, the white poor child would still be considered less oppressed because, no matter what other identities you have, being white is the ultimate trump card.

Just like the unofficial racial oppression hierarchy, the value of these different intersecting identities can fluctuate based on whatever is the most convenient argument to make in the moment.

I want to note that normal human beings (hopefully like the ones reading this book) would not view competing for oppression points as a positive thing, but sadly that's exactly what the woke do. It's like collecting tickets at an arcade when you're a kid—for every category they fall into and declare publicly, they get more tickets as if they are competing for the largest prize. Look at their bios on social media. You'll see their pronouns (lots of ones that are not she/her or he/him) alongside a list of other intersecting characteristics: bipolar, fat, queer, and so on. They brag about it because the more oppression you experience, the more other people are supposed to treat you as a victim of the system and coddle your every need and desire.

Another way to look at it is that the more oppression points you experience, the more positive attention you get from the woke. It's how they gain social status and standing.

## When Opportunity Arises, Oppression Changes

It's important to note that this hierarchy sometimes shifts, and groups who are generally considered low on the oppression scale can vault their way up to the top depending on what the woke find most advantageous to enhance their agenda.

Let's take the very confusing case of Asians, for instance. Generally speaking, the woke do not consider Asians to be oppressed. In fact, if we're looking for instances of systemic racism, we can look no further than elite colleges like Harvard, Yale, and Princeton where they actively discriminate against Asians in their admissions processes, holding them to higher academic standards for acceptance than any other population based purely on their skin color.

However, when the COVID pandemic first hit, Asians made a comeback and shot right up to the top of the oppression hierarchy. Why? Because early on in the crisis, Donald Trump restricted travel from China (a move that even Dr. Anthony Fauci had to admit was ultimately the correct call, and probably saved a lot of lives). As a thank you, the woke left framed the Asian community as oppressed victims to have a new reason to call Trump a racist.

After a few months of declaring that everyone who correctly pointed out that COVID came from China was a racist (or CHY-NA, as Trump would say to troll them), the news cycle changed with the death of George Floyd and shifted the conversation to Black Lives Matter. Like magic, Asians dropped back down to their normal place in the hierarchy. They were no longer considered oppressed, or at least not as oppressed as they were prior to Floyd's death.

We saw this happen again a year later in March 2021 when a mentally ill individual with a sex addiction shot up several massage parlors in Atlanta, killing several Asian employees. The woke love nothing more than to jump on a tragedy for their own political gain. Suddenly, Asian oppression at the hands of a deeply racist society dominated the news cycles, and the Stop Asian Hate campaign swung into high gear in order to combat hate crimes directed at this obviously oppressed community. Calls of white supremacy and systemic racism were made in major newspapers and all over cable news!

However, there was just one problem: according to the FBI, the majority of hate crimes against Asian Americans are not committed by white people. They're committed by African American men. But to point out that demographic reality would have broken the hierarchy, and so the news kept it quiet. There was one article in the *Washington Post* about an attack on an older Asian lady in New York City by a black man that happened right out in front of a swanky apartment complex as the building security looked on and did nothing. The article featured video of the attack, showing clearly the perpetrator was black. However, the article never once mentioned his race. You see, no matter how oppressed the woke consider Asians to be at any given time, they can never surpass the oppression that black people face in this system.

And that leads us to our next lesson about the hierarchy: the woke believe that you can't be racist to people if they experience more oppression than you do.

## It's All About Power

We've already established that the woke changed the definition of racism to make it about the system rather than the individual.

However, that's not all they did. They also made power a part of the racism equation.

Traditionally, we think of racism as one individual or group having prejudice towards another. You may also think of it as stereotyping or scapegoating a group based on their race with negative connotations.

We need to be honest that, in addition to the obvious example of slavery, our country's history is littered with examples of true racial injustices that occurred in the lifetimes of people alive today. White store owners in the South not allowing black patrons to sit at lunch counters was a form of prejudice—it held one group to a different standard of treatment based purely on the color of their skin. Segregation in schools was prejudice. Redlining, which denied services to black Americans to prevent them from living in certain neighborhoods, was prejudice. We can all agree that those things were bad and be thankful that we have progressed beyond them.

But what happens when solving "racism" means embracing an equity mindset that says, "From each according to their ability, to each according to their need"?

It means that they are going to attempt to prioritize the resources allocated to groups based on their oppression level in order to level the playing field. The more oppressed you are, the more resources you get. And they are trying to implement a system where it will be administered and managed by the state.

Here are a few examples of how this plays out in the real world:

- In 2019, the New York City Department of Education was sued for $90 million after the schools chancellor began a crusade to rid the department of "toxic whiteness," which included demoting white employees purely based on skin color so that non-white employees could take their spots.
- After the death of George Floyd, UCLA Professor Gordon Klein was suspended by the university and placed under police protection after getting death threats. His crime was refusing to exempt black students (and only black students) from their exams. UCLA is a public, taxpayer-funded university.
- Joe Biden openly bragged that he was going to prioritize a black female running mate during his presidential campaign, meaning that Kamala Harris was only selected for the job based on her immutable characteristics. (We all know it wasn't because she was the best campaigner or even the best choice for the job she ultimately ended up holding.)

Some might call these actions of giving individuals advantages based purely on their skin color *racist*.

The 1964 Civil Rights Act forbids discrimination on the basis of race, color, religion, sex, or national origin. It doesn't say on the basis of race *except* if you're white. It says on the basis of race.

One could argue that a state agency like the Department of Education making employment decisions to demote white employees purely based on skin color is racist.

One could argue that a state-funded university making decisions that benefit black students without applying those standards equally to every other group is racist.

And one could argue that selecting a vice president of the United States based purely on the color of her skin and gender is racist and misandry.

All those people would be correct—that is why the woke updated the definition of racism to include a qualifier: "*racism = power + prejudice.*"

Here's what this means: you cannot be racist towards groups that have more power than you do based on the oppression hierarchy.

Let's look at that hierarchy again. Remember, the closer to the top of the list, the more oppression you experience. The closer you are to the bottom of the list, the more power you have.

- Black
- Native Americans
- Latino/Hispanic
- Asians
- Jews
- White

When you add "power" into the definition of racism and combine it with who the woke believe have power, suddenly black people can never be racist towards any other group, and no one can ever be racist towards white people.

This is why news outlets were reporting that hate crimes against Asians were on the rise after the Atlanta shooting but labeled it as white supremacy instead of pointing out the statistics from the FBI that showed that the majority of hate crimes against Asians were committed by black people. In the woke hierarchy, it is literally impossible for black people to be racist towards Asians since they will always outrank them on the hierarchy.

It's also why they claim that it is impossible for white people to experience racism at all. Remember, the argument for systemic racism is that white people created a system that would only benefit other white people to maintain power exclusively for people who looked like them. The argument follows that if white people hold all the power, they can't possibly be discriminated against on the basis of their skin color.

Of course, that's rubbish. If someone makes a judgement about you based purely on the color of your skin without regard for the content of your character, that is racism. The only reason to argue for a standard of racism to include a subjective judgment about the power a group holds is if you want to actively discriminate against a specific group of people.

This is exactly what the woke want to do. They actively want to discriminate against white people as retribution and revenge for what they perceive as an irredeemably racist history of the United States.

In 2020, the state of California had Proposition 16 on their ballot: support a constitutional amendment to *REPEAL* Proposition 209 (1996), which stated that the government and public institutions cannot discriminate against, or grant preferential treatment to, persons on the basis of race, sex, color, ethnicity, or national origin in public employment, public education, or public contracting.

Yes, you just read that the state of California was trying to *repeal* a constitutional amendment that prevents discrimination on the basis of race. Why would they do that? Why would it be so critical to get rid of an amendment that says they can't discriminate? Because they want to discriminate on the basis of race, and I'll give you three guesses about which groups they want to be able to target.

*"I'm sorry, we're currently not hiring white men, but if you want to complete gender reassignment surgery, you'll be more than welcome to apply."*

(I'm being facetious, of course. OK, not really.)

Luckily, even this idea was a step too far for the state's residents, and it was defeated in the election.

## You Can't Solve Racism with More Racism

Listen, I'm not one of those people who will complain about how hard it is to be white in America today. That's simply not the truth. There are absolutely realities that we still need to deal with when it comes to race in this country to truly ensure that everyone, regardless of their skin color, has access to every opportunity they could ever dream of. We have an obligation to live up to the promise of the American dream, and we're not there yet.

However, it can be true that there are still racial disparities to work through in this country—and it can ALSO be true that the woke mob on the progressive left isn't really interested in solving racism as much as they are interested in using black

Americans to gain more power for themselves, win elections, and enact their "anti-racist" policy to create a little equitable utopia.

In the very first part of the very first chapter of this book, I told you that a focus on racism wasn't happening by accident. It was a deliberate effort by every major institution to keep us divided and fighting each other rather than focusing on them. To accomplish that goal, they took advantage of this destructive ideology.

Every aim this ideology has is cultural revolution.

It's ironic, because even though the woke occasionally boost Asians in the oppression hierarchy, the truth is that Chinese Americans are some of the fiercest opponents of Critical Race Theory. Why? Because many of them lived during Mao Zedong's Cultural Revolution in China or have parents who did. They know what it looks like and know that it is exactly what we are seeing happen in the United States.

That's the more important thing you need to learn about the woke ideology: It's not really about race. It's about revolution.

They're simply using race as the fastest way to accelerate the destruction of our systems, our institutions, our values, and our way of life.

And that should make every single American afraid enough to want to do something to fight back.

# The Woke Mind in the Wild

I was a Democrat for twenty years, from the time I was eighteen years old up until the day of the New Hampshire primary in 2020 when I was thirty-eight years old. That's when I accidentally went viral on the internet for writing a confession about having been a Democrat who attended a Trump rally (just google my name and "Trump rally"; I promise it'll pop right up). The experiences I outlined earlier in this book—the knitting wars and my friends turning into pod people—were just a few of the things that led me on the path to that Trump rally.

I tell you this not to revisit the story of how I woke up. Instead, I want to talk about why I think I avoided becoming woke myself.

Because it was a damn miracle I didn't become woke. I could have very easily fallen down the same trap door as my friends did, and I've given a lot of thought as to why I didn't. I truly consider it an intervention from God that I didn't follow in their footsteps and become woke myself.

## Make MySpace Great Again

Fun fact: I used to run one of the most popular political blogs on MySpace. This was before Facebook opened up their registration to everyone, and MySpace was the place to be back then.

I was a smart-ass who knew absolutely nothing, but I listened to Air America all day (Sam Seder was my favorite… can't stand him now), was obsessed with progressive politics, and constantly put my thoughts out on the platform for public consumption.

A lot of people don't remember this, but back during the George W. Bush years, around 2004/2005, MySpace had an awesome blogging platform, with ratings and popularity lists that made it easy to have your content discovered. I was ranked in the top of the news and politics section almost every day of the week. I would get over 250,000 views a month just by blogging politics on MySpace. It was wild.

Then came Obama. I lived in Norwich, Vermont, at the time, about a mile away from the New Hampshire border, and so I had easy access to campaign events for the first in the nation (FITN) primary. I saw Obama in person several times and voted for him enthusiastically. When he got elected, I didn't have anything to complain about anymore. I think his election made me feel relieved, like I didn't have to worry every day about what was going on in the country. It was like a switch to politics turned off in my brain, and it stayed off for both of his terms in office.

With the benefit of hindsight, that was exactly what the Democrats wanted, wasn't it? They wanted to rile you up with fear over the previous administration (OK, let's be honest, I still don't think W was a great president) and then help you fall back asleep when they are back in power.

In July 2021, the White House teamed up with CNN to put on a live town hall with Joe Biden. Pictures from the back of the room later surfaced that showed most of the seats were empty. That means the corporate media has done such a good job of putting the people who voted for Biden back to sleep that they couldn't even muster up enough interest to give away a few hundred tickets to a live town hall event airing on their favorite news network. Just think about that for a second—this is supposedly the president who got the most votes of any in history. They know what they're doing, I'll give them that.

Anyway, after Obama took office, life went on. I moved around, worked different jobs, bought a house, got married, finished graduate school, and started my own organizational psychology practice. I paid very little attention to politics and, when I did, I was always watching left-leaning news. And what's more, I did it purposefully. I had absolutely no interest in objective coverage. I was only listening to people I knew I would mostly agree with. By the time 2016 came around, I would mostly watch MSNBC in my house.

So, I was absolutely shocked when Trump won. I did not see it coming in the slightest bit.

I remember sitting on my couch on election night drinking a bottle of champagne to celebrate the election of the first female president...until it all started going horribly wrong. Every moment that went by, more dread started to course through me. I went to bed early with a pit in my stomach and, sure enough, when I opened the news the next day, I saw the words I dreaded most: Trump had won.

I cried. Yes, I was that guy. The first few days after that were ROUGH. I was truly angry about what had happened, and my anger wasn't directed at the news media that had lied to me—it was directed at the new president-elect.

But I had a few trump cards up my sleeve, if you will. I had the ability to shift my perspective, looking at things that might seem like the worst thing ever and learning how to use them to my advantage. The second card was spirituality, or a belief in something higher than myself.

When I first started my organizational psychology practice, I hired a life coach named Joshua MacGuire to help me maintain my focus and perspective. (Yes, the same Joshua who is on my YouTube channel once a week these days!) I had been working with Joshua for almost a year with the purpose of maintaining a positive mindset so that my business could have the best chance of being successful. I know that I'm my own worst enemy, and I knew early on that maintaining my mindset was the difference between success and failure. Joshua was (and still is) vital to keeping me focused on the things that matter most.

A few days after the election when I was so upset about what happened, I distinctly remember him saying, "Karlyn, you just don't know. Maybe this will be the best thing that could have happened."

I'm not sure he knew how correct that prediction would be at the time.

Joshua is a psychic. Yes, I said psychic. I really do believe in that stuff. I always have, but working with him led me to a whole new understanding of life and spirituality and energy and all things woo-woo. I know many of you probably don't believe in that stuff, but freedom means the freedom to believe in things other people think are crazy.

And it was this crazy woo-woo stuff that led me right to the second thing that prevented me from going woke: a spiritual retreat to Peru a few weeks after the election where I did ayahuasca and San Pedro with a group of people at a remote spiritual center for ten days. I mean really—if Donald Trump was going to be president, why not go do psychedelics with a group of strangers in the jungle as a way to cope? Nothing could have gone wrong with this plan.

This ended up being one of the most impactful experiences of my life. I came home with a connection to God that I hadn't experienced in my entire life. It woke up my intuition and actually made me a much better psychologist because it was much easier to pick up on different emotional nuances of any given situation. That meant I was better able to read the solutions to all sorts of people problems.

More importantly, it made Trump seem so small. Listen, I had been shown the secrets of the universe by "Mama Ayahuasca"; why would a silly thing like who's president hold me down? I even started finding humor in Trump. If we were going to be stuck in this position for four years, why not find some joy in it?

I truly believe it was these two attributes—a generally optimistic mindset and a highly spiritualized experience where I connected personally with God—that saved me from being woke. In fact, I'd go so far as to call it divine intervention.

In this chapter, I'll explore the most prominent characteristics that I see when interacting with the woke. We have to know who they are and what they're motivated by if we're going to triumph over them (and maybe even wake a few of them up along the way).

## Some Perspectives Are More Woke Than Others

Let's be clear: doing ayahuasca in a jungle is probably not the right solution for everyone to avoid being taken over by the woke mind virus. Certainly, there are many people in the world who are not woke and don't have a religious or spiritual practice.

However, I do believe there's something to be said about a generally positive, forward-looking perspective. All too often, when you talk to the woke, they are so focused on everything they don't like in the world that they forget to acknowledge all the things that are great.

In my experience, there are two types of people in the world: creators and destroyers.

- *Creators* are people who give value to the world. They are more likely to take personal responsibility for the things they experience in life and appreciate opportunities, tending to do a better job of taking advantage of them when they are presented. Creators believe in themselves and what they are able to contribute, which is why they are more likely to create things that are of value. That's not to say creators can't have bad days—they can. But, generally speaking, they focus their energy on building things up rather than tearing them down.
- *Destroyers* are just the opposite. The thing about destroyers is that they don't think much of themselves.

> The value we give to the world reflects how we feel about ourselves—if you don't have high self-worth, why would you believe that you have anything to contribute to the world? Instead of seeking validation internally, they look to others to define their value in the world. And when they don't receive what they are seeking, they tend to focus their energy on destroying the work of others rather than creating something of their own.

A bit overly simplistic, sure, but I generally find that you can tell if someone is a creator or a destroyer within a conversation or two. A really simple test is to trust your intuition. Our intuition comes from somewhere—it's our brain processing eleven million pieces of information every single second (all but forty of which are in your subconscious) and delivering you an answer without telling how it got there. Another term for that is a gut instinct.

If you want to know if someone is a creator or a destroyer, just ask yourself this question: Does talking to the person make you feel good?

Or you could try any of these variations: Does this person inspire you? Do they make you want to be better? Do they make you happy? Do they genuinely make you laugh?

If you answered yes, chances are you're talking to a creator. Because they focus on giving value to the world, creators just tend to be a lot more pleasant to be around than destroyers. There is something about when a person has self-confidence and knows they can achieve on their own, they tend to put others at ease around them because they are not threatened by them.

Next question: What do you think the woke are more likely to be? Creators or destroyers?

We could probably answer that question simply by considering the sheer volume of property and businesses that were destroyed in the Black Lives Matter riots in the summer of 2020—over $2 billion of damage. Some argued that the destruction was merely a form of reparations that they were owed for sins of the past.

But that's not the only reason to believe that the woke trend more towards being destroyers than they do creators. Let's look at the comparison of equality (equality of opportunity) to equity (equality of outcomes) that we covered in the previous chapter.

People who believe in equality know that nothing is guaranteed to them—they have to show up and work hard to earn it.

People who believe in equity fundamentally believe that we should all end up in the same place, without taking individual effort into consideration in their calculations.

People who believe in equality are probably more likely to feel gratitude and appreciation for the opportunities that they are given—be it a chance to go to college, a good job offer, or even just another person doing them a favor. That gratitude helps make them more likely to take advantage of those opportunities.

People who believe in equity expect these opportunities to be given to them. They expect free college, free healthcare, a fifteen-dollar-an-hour minimum wage, and a universal basic income. The sad truth is that they are less likely to appreciate any of it.

And so on, and so forth. The bottom line is this: something that is given has no value, and a goal that is easy to achieve doesn't offer as much fulfillment and satisfaction as a goal that is hard to achieve when it's attained.

Creators seek opportunities with appreciation.

Destroyers demand outcomes and blame everyone but themselves when they don't get what they want.

## They've Been Invaded by a Mind Virus

I joke that the first time I read *White Fragility*, I descended into madness. Except that it's not entirely a joke—there is truth in it. I distinctly remember getting about halfway into that book when I felt like I was seriously losing myself in it. It was just so insane! Every page, my jaw would drop a little more.

And then I thought about all the people who pick up this content because they genuinely think it's what they need to do in order to be a good person. They read it seriously, not thinking critically enough about it to question why they're reading a book written by a white lady who admits she is a racist.

Though it is difficult to know anyone's true intentions, I do believe that most of the people who are sucked in by the woke are doing it with positive ones. In fact, they are victims of the situation as much as the people they ultimately victimize. Some of you know the feeling of being told by every person in your life that not only is this what you need to do to be a good person, but you also need to do it to be accepted by them. In situations like this, the path of least resistance is to just give in and go along with it.

It's important to keep this context in mind. As we work our way through this chapter, you'll see that people who get sucked into this ideology are very broken people and are surrounding themselves with other broken people to create an echo chamber that reinforces the collective beliefs of everyone involved.

There is something about the woke ideology that is truly evil. I'm generally not a person who calls things demonic, but in this case, I don't know a better way to explain how I perceive its effect on people. It's a heavy, dark, angry view of the world that seems to completely infiltrate and take over the very beings of the people infected. It makes good people do bad things. It changes their attitudes, perspectives, behaviors, and even their physical appearance changes.

And it's no wonder why. This ideology slowly infiltrates by planting one crazy idea, repeating it enough to convince the recipient, and then moves on to the next crazy idea.

Here's a sample of some of the things the woke believe:

- *Immutable characteristics are the most interesting thing about a person*. They truly believe that the color of your skin, gender, or sexual orientation are the defining elements of any individual human experience. While no one would deny those things are important, the prominence of its importance is up to every person, not the will of a vocal collectivist minority.
- *Segregation is a good thing*. Internal records show that the City of Seattle held segregated employee training sessions in which white employees were asked to come in on a scheduled holiday and attend one training, while non-white employees attended a completely separate session. This is a very common practice when Critical Race Theory is integrated in the workplace or in university settings. Do a quick search on YouTube

of "white people talking to white people about racism" and you'll see what I mean.

- *Black people don't know how to get an ID.* The woke are vehemently against voter ID laws. They claim it disenfranchises voters while the right believes they're using it as a loophole to cheat their way to victory. However, from my perspective, it doesn't matter if it's nefarious or benevolent: the basic premise—that voter ID laws are racist—means that they truly believe that black people are incapable of going to the DMV and getting an ID! That is an incredibly racist idea. By the way, they also believe that hard work, capitalism, and Christianity are also components of white supremacy.
- *White people are the norm, and non-white people are abnormal.* I've watched thousands of hours of diversity training programs based on Critical Race Theory that have been used in real organizations, and one of the most disturbing things I hear consistently is this idea that anti-racism is necessary because white people consider themselves to be the "norm" or the "default." The thing is that I've only ever heard anti-racist trainers referring to white people as the "norm," which means they are projecting their own racist attitudes onto all of us.
- *Human beings are merely "bodies."* Another disturbing (and also very revealing) component that consistently comes up in diversity trainings is the idea of referring to minorities as "black and brown bodies." The simple idea of referring to someone as a "body" instead of a person seems to take away their very humanity. The

"oppressed" people, instead, become a tool that is to be used for the trainer's purposes.

- *You fix racism by creating more racism*. The Critical Race theorists argue that the Civil Rights Movement didn't go far enough. They believe that equality was not the correct goal, and that they should have gone further and demanded revenge in the form of various sanctions to make things "equal." That means they believe that the solution to racism is literally more racism—it's racism in reverse for the purposes of leveling the playing field.

## They're Addicted to Negative Emotions

In a world where the majority of people are addicted to outrage, a truly happy, normal person looks insane.

Human beings can become addicted to emotions. I see this in the workplace all the time: A person hates their boss. Every day they come in, their boss does something to piss them off, they get angry, and so they have a horrible rest of their day.

Then, something interesting happens when their boss goes on vacation for a week. The first few days they come into the office, they feel great! It's a new world! The boss isn't there to piss them off, and they can actually focus on their work.

But something interesting happens on day three or four of the boss's vacation—the employee starts to create problems where none existed. They might get angry at the perceived tone of an email from a colleague, or get offended if a subordinate looked at them the wrong way in a one-on-one meeting. They make a mountain out of a molehill if the slightest thing goes wrong, blowing it out of proportion entirely.

This happens because, over time, that employee has become addicted to the negative emotions. Every single time their boss pissed them off in the past, they had an emotional reaction to it that translated into their brain pushing all sorts of stress-producing hormones into their body. The body got addicted to the act of getting that influx of stress-producing hormones every single day when the boss was in the office, just like one gets addicted to cigarettes, alcohol, or drugs. If the body doesn't get its fix, it starts to go through withdrawal. But the cure for withdrawal from negative emotions is simple—just find something new to be angry about. When human beings want to be angry, they can always find a reason.

The woke are very angry people.

With the true believers in the woke ideology, it becomes impossible for them to live without being on a constant lookout for opportunities to call out racism and get their good little ally points. Robin DiAngelo even encourages this in her work, teaching that co-workers should call each other out anytime they register a grievance for the slightest infraction.

In the 1950s, Hans Selye did pioneer research into the impact of stress on the body, developing the concept of General Adaptation Syndrome (yes, the acronym is GAS). When our body experiences stress, we first have a fight-or-flight response where we either fight the stressor directly, or we run away from it as fast as we can. If that doesn't work and the stress continues, our body actively begins to fight the stress, reallocating our physical and emotional resources to getting rid of the problem. Finally, prolonged exposure to the stressor will deplete the body's resources, resulting in physical illness. This might be something minor like a headache—or it might be something major, like a heart attack.

Negative emotions have a physical impact on the body over time, and we are raising an entire generation of woke activists who are addicted to negative emotions. This is learned behavior that is being taught to younger and younger audiences. And it's making them sick.

A report that was released in July 2020 shared that the rate of depression of undergraduate students at Harvard University had risen almost ten points between 2014 and 2018, increasing from 22 percent to 31 percent. The percent with anxiety disorder increased from 19 percent to 30 percent. And the proportion of undergraduates at Harvard who reported suicidal ideation increased from 4 percent to 6 percent.

Think about that for a moment. These are students at the most elite school in the world. They had to be better than 99 percent of the population to get into that school. They have access to all of the resources they could ever need. They are virtually guaranteed a good job upon graduation. And don't worry, they are in a place that is going more and more woke by the day. With anti-racism statements all over the place and one of the largest diversity staffs on the planet, Harvard is the ultimate safe space.

So, at this elite institution that checks every box, why are depression, anxiety, and suicidal ideation rates going up?

It could be that we've trained an entire generation to constantly be on the lookout for things they don't like in this world—things that are "problematic," if you will. When you develop a habit of constantly looking for the negative in life, you will only ever see things to be upset about. Eventually, this will turn into an addiction to anger and outrage. They will struggle to live life without feeding that addiction.

This also aligns with trends we see regarding the connection between political affiliation and mental health.

A study conducted by ADoH Scientific, released in November 2020, reported that Democrats had roughly 71 percent higher stress levels than Republicans and nearly twice the anxiety levels (92 percent higher). They also reported being 35 percent lonelier than Republicans and feeling 69 percent more irritable. This was corroborated by a second study, also released in 2020, from Pew Research Center's American Trends Panel that found that conservatives are significantly less likely to be diagnosed with mental health issues that those who identify as either liberal or very liberal.

"Well, that was obviously because of the 2020 election, Karlyn. That was the most stressful election of our lifetime, especially for Democrats!"

OK, sure. But let me take you on a trip back to May 2013, not long after Barack Obama had been sworn in for a second term. BuzzFeed partnered with Survey Monkey to conduct a study of Americans' mental health based on their political affiliation. Here's what they found: Democrats were 2 percent more likely to have bipolar disorder, 4 percent more likely to experience post-traumatic stress disorder, 5 percent more likely to have ADD/ADHD, 10 percent more likely to experience anxiety, and 11 percent more likely to experience depression.

Now, I am not suggesting that everyone on the political left is unhappy, unfulfilled, or experiences mental illness. That's not true. Keep in mind, there are varying degrees of this: not every person who buys into the woke ideology is angry all the time.

But the activists—the people driving the culture change we are seeing in the world today—tend to exhibit this trait. They wear their anger all over their face. It is palatable. These are the ones you'll encounter most commonly, the true believers.

## They Are Schemers

When the pandemic first started in early 2020, the woke got pretty quiet. It was so nice! They didn't disappear entirely (remember, it was still considered racist to point out that COVID came from China), but they were much less active than usual. I chalked it up to there being a legitimate problem in the world, one they couldn't deny or escape from.

The woke like to use the phrase "problematic" to describe actions, things, or people they don't like, but the fact is that nine times out of ten, they are not describing things the average person would consider a real problem. We're talking things like white people eating sushi (cultural appropriation), the name of the Washington Redskins (cultural appropriation AND racism), or the backlash against Meghan Markle for making accusations against the royal family (racism AND sexism). All of these problems pale in comparison to a worldwide pandemic that has shut down the entire economy.

So, the woke went undercover and regrouped. Then, after a few months of being cooped up during the lockdowns and unemployment, George Floyd tragically died.

And before a funeral had taken place, the woke shot out of a canon and into the streets for months of protests (as well as looting, rioting, creating autonomous zones in major cities with no repercussion, and defunding the police). It all resulted in a sharp increase in violent crime in major cities and over $2 billion of property damage.

It is true that George Floyd's death was a tragedy. Some people believe he died of a drug overdose, others believe he was murdered at the hands of police. I think that regardless of whether he overdosed or not, the police still behaved grossly irresponsibly. I also believe that dying of a drug overdose is just as much of a tragedy as dying of murder. The pain of that loss doesn't hurt less for the people who loved him just because the cause is different.

So, his death was a tragedy. And certainly, there were people who participated in the protests that ensued afterwards who did it for the right reasons. For many of them, that was probably true. You could argue that they were just virtue signaling, but a virtue signal is not the worst crime the woke commit by a long shot.

However, it can also be true that his death was taken advantage of by nefarious actors to advance a political agenda. Police departments were defunded across the country. Black Lives Matter raised more than $90 million. The Democrats used it to discredit Trump during his reelection bid.

They did all of this in the face of any logic and reason, because the very last thing you want to do in the middle of a supposedly deadly, highly contagious pandemic is gather hundreds of thousands of people together to protest. Anyone who dared question why these very large groups of people were suddenly insusceptible to the virus were called white supremacists and were told racism is a public health crisis that is worse than the virus.

The woke uses tragedies all the time when it's convenient to advance their political goals. They will use any high profile story to their advantage and many lower profile ones as well. Always remember that their goal is not to achieve a fair and just world—their goal is to destabilize society. When you reverse engineer their actions from that goal, it tells you all you need to know about whether the intent behind those actions was nefarious or pure.

## They Are the Bulls in the China Shop

As an organizational psychologist, I use the DISC model in workplace trainings, mostly because I've found it the easiest to teach and apply to the most common situations in the working world. DISC stands for "Dominant, Influence, Steadiness, and Conscientiousness," and every person is made up of a combination of those styles. If you work with DISC long enough, it becomes very easy to "people-read" when you encounter people based on their behavior, so you learn to identify quickly who is what style.

A common theme I have noticed in the woke is that their behaviors tend to align with the most rigid work styles (Dominant and Conscientiousness) as opposed to the more flexible, open ones (Influence and Steady).

There are several commonalities between the woke and people who tend to gravitate to the "D" and "C" styles:

- *It's their way or the highway*: They have authoritarian tendencies and can feel very uncomfortable when they are taken out of control or are asked to do something a different way.
- *They love a good fight*: While "I" and "S" styles tend to want to dive under a chair and hide when there is conflict, the "D" and "C" styles can get revved up by it. They love a good debate.

- *They think they are the smartest in the room*: A point of pride for many of the woke, particularly those with more of the "C" style in them, is that they are the person who's never wrong. They were the kid in school who refused to raise their hand unless they were 110 percent certain they were right.
- *They're not afraid to piss people off*: Not only do they not care what you think of their methods, they might try to piss you off just to prove they can. It's a way of gaining power over you.

But scariest of all, they believe that the ends justify their means. They are not going to behave ethically or fight fair because they truly believe that their goal of equity is worthy enough to leave a trail of destruction in its wake.

Without naming names, let's just say there are a lot of anti-woke intellectuals who truly believe that we can intellectualize our way out of this problem with a good reasonable conversation and discussion. They have highly civilized debates about the downfall of western civilization and then go out for brandy and smoke cigars to congratulate themselves on how intellectually smart they are.

In reality, this is not going to work. The woke do not want to have a reasonable conversation. They see the world in black and white; they want to fight, they're really good at it, and they want to win. They are truly terrified of what losing power means for them, many times even seeing it as a literal matter of life and death.

We are up against a group of people who have an absolute belief that they are the smartest person in the conversation, that everyone who disagrees with them is an idiot anyway, and that their goals are the worthiest causes in the history of humanity. They also refuse to look at any data that contradicts their current world view. That is an impossible fight to intellectualize. You cannot have a reasonable conversation with someone who is unwilling to have a reasonable conversation with you.

It's not impossible to have conversations with the woke, and maybe even drop in a golden nugget or two along the way, but it is very rare. We need to be honest about this.

## Racism Is Their God

I'm not a person who believes there is any true religion that works for anyone and everyone—I think people find God in their own ways when (and if) they're ready. And if they're an atheist, that's fine, too, so long as there's a positive focus of energy towards creating value in the world.

However, I believe the most susceptible group to go woke on the political left are those who do not have a spiritual practice of some sort and are not focusing their energy towards creating value, leaving them open to be a destroyer instead of a creator. Human beings are naturally explorers, inventors, and creators. When we are not focusing our energy productively, it leaves a void in our experience that needs to be filled by something.

With a lack of any sort of higher purpose, the only higher purpose the woke left have is fighting the evils of racism. Therefore, racism is at the center of their existence. It is their purpose. They worship it, make it the centerpiece of their worlds, even give glory to it by raising a Black Lives Matter fist in the air and swearing allegiance to it. In the weeks following

George Floyd's death, photos and videos surfaced of religious (almost cult-like) rituals that included white people washing the feet of black people, apologizing on bended knee for being born white, and even kissing the shoes of black people who asked them to as reparations.

Let's play this out to its most logical conclusion: Do you really believe the woke want to solve racism when they have very literally made it the center of their experience?

Or asking it a different way, for the religious and spiritual people reading this book: Would you actively work to kill off the God of your belief system?

The answer to both is no. If they killed off their God, what other purpose would they have in their lives?

In fact, I would argue that not only do they not want to solve racism—their actions have actually created more racism.

Some people believe that Critical Race Theory is an anti-white ideology. If you see a group of white people being pressured into kneeling down and kissing a stranger's shoe purely because of the color of their skin, we can understand that! However, I believe that's both overly simplistic and dangerous at the same time.

Here's why it's overly simplistic: Critical Race Theory is racist against everyone. We've already explored just a few instances of how CRT is racist against the groups it calls oppressed—believing black people can't get an ID or not acknowledging who's really committing the anti-Asian hate crimes are just a few examples. Although there are absolutely components that impact white people, you could also argue that the ideology is overly white supremacist, believing that white people are the norm, the default, and top of society. Lastly, remember that the goal of CRT has nothing to do with race—race is simply a tool used to destabilize society so that they can rebuild it in the image of Marx. It's not about race—it's about power.

Here's why it's dangerous: life is about balance. If the pendulum swings too far in one direction, human beings have an incredible way of swinging it back, be it consciously or unconsciously. As the public becomes more aware of what Critical Race Theory is, many of the commentators discussing it are choosing to present it as a battle of black versus white. That's leading people who are just being introduced to this incredibly complicated ideology to believe that it's simply against white people. They don't understand the nuance. And I am truly afraid that this is going to lead to the creation of a legitimate white power movement.

I've been personally attacked by mobs of thousands of white identitarians for refusing to call CRT "anti-white" publicly. They demanded I support their movement, calling it "white wellbeing," "white positivity," and even "white survival." These are dangerous people, and they are actively using the actions of the woke left to recruit for their very real identitarian movement.

And this is possibly the greatest proof that racism is their one true God. In a time when the KKK is virtually dead in the United States, the woke wanted racism to exist so badly that they literally created it out of thin air.

They conjured up their perfect enemy. They wanted people to be more racist, declared half of the country to be racist, got them canceled on social media for being racist, and got them fired from their jobs for being racist. They were pushed into more extreme corners of the internet where they were only interacting with people who had been banned on the main-stream platforms.

The woke left worship racism so deeply that they are creating more racism through their direct actions.

## They Don't Believe Success Is Possible

In a July 2021 workshop, the foremost expert on the woke in the world, James Lindsay, was asked what can wake up the woke. He replied that they needed to be given the gifts of responsibility and accountability. Once given that, they would start a positive feedback loop to reinforce the fundamentally different direction.

Another way to say this might be that the woke need to get a job. Although we'll find out later that corporate America has embraced the woke, so that might not even be good enough.

The woke live in a constant state of entitlement. They feel entitled to have constant conformity with their views by the people around them, entitled to safe spaces where they'll never be challenged, and entitled to government programs to fund their education, health care, and even day-to-day living expenses. They not only feel entitled to police and "call out" the behavior of others they don't like, they also feel entitled to demand adherence to certain thoughts. Yes, thoughtcrime as described in George Orwell's *1984* is now a real thing.

Why might one feel so entitled to the hard work, efforts, and resources of others?

If we think about the root cause, it's probably because they haven't been taught that they have the ability to do it on their own. If you thought you could do it on your own then why would you need someone else to do it for you?

Positive psychologist Michelle Gielan has explored the idea of a success mindset. She argues there are three components that will lead to success in your career, but these ideas are more broadly applicable as well:

1. *Optimism*: The belief that success is possible and that your actions matter in the face of a challenge.
2. *Positive Engagement*: Looking at stress as a positive challenge rather than something to be feared.
3. *Support Provision*: A propensity to help the people around you.

Now, let's compare these attributes to a few generalizations we can make about the woke:

1. *Optimism*: The woke argue that equity (equality of outcomes) is the goal rather than equality of opportunity. If they don't believe hard work really matters because they believe that a person's success is determined by their immutable characteristics, *how could they believe that an individual's actions matter in the face of a challenge?*
2. *Positive Engagement*: One of the most pronounced desires of the woke mobs is safe spaces: areas where they will never be challenged in any way. If they've never learned how to manage stress and work through it, *how can they possibly look at it as a positive challenge when they encounter it in life?*
3. *Support Provision*: A common saying you will hear among the woke is that they expect to be paid for their emotional labor. That is, they expect compensation

> anytime they have to explain anything to anyone and will actively tell their white allies that they shouldn't expect them to take the time to educate you. *Does that sound like a group of people that would be open to helping others?*

We can argue about the cause of all this—the parents, the educational system, our culture in general. But regardless of the root cause, the incredibly sad reality is that we have an entire population that doesn't believe in their own ability to be successful based on their merit. And the more oppression points you have, the less chance of success you have in the real world.

In many cases, they have been taught they can't be successful because of the color of their skin, their gender, or other immutable characteristics, and it's come from the people they trusted to show them the way in life. If you've been taught that the entire system is working against you because of something you can't control, then why would you have an optimistic outlook? They haven't been taught to in a meaningful way!

People get this wrong about the woke: They believe that because they act entitled, it's because their confidence and self-esteem is too high. They say they've been coddled by the adults in their lives so much that they have huge, overinflated egos!

But it's really the opposite. Their self-esteem isn't too high. It is virtually undeveloped. That is why they are constantly looking for other people to validate their reality and have learned to look for self-worth in things and achievements outside of themselves, which is why they are constantly making demands of others. They don't make demands because they feel good about themselves—it is the opposite. They make demands because they don't feel they are worthy of getting what they want any other way.

Confidence and self-esteem come from being true to yourself, to your desires, and pursuing them unapologetically. It comes from getting knocked down, getting back up again, and feeling the fulfillment that comes from the process of achieving success. It comes from learning to be happy with what you're doing right now rather than waiting to achieve some arbitrary milestone in life.

## Many of Them Don't Know What They're Doing

I've painted a very bleak picture in this chapter of the type of person you can expect to encounter when you're fighting the woke. But I want to offer a bit of good news: many of them truly believe they are doing it for the right reasons.

The woke will tell you that anyone who is a Republican or a Trump supporter (or anyone, really, who's to the right of Mao) is an alt-right extremist and a racist. They would have you believe that seventy-four million people in this country are alt-right extremists. That's simply not true.

But it's also not true that everyone in the Democratic Party or on the political left are part of the angry, unreasonable, woke army. Most of them are just trying to do the best they can and truly believe they are participating in this to achieve positive outcomes for more people. Many estimates I've seen place the number of woke in the overall population at around 12 percent, but admittedly that may have expanded in 2020, and it's a difficult thing to measure in an accurate way.

That means that most people are on our side, it's just that many of them don't realize it. They are not bad people; they are just being influenced to do bad things and support bad policies by nefarious actors. They are being lied to by the media just as much as many of us were, and in order to win, we need to wake more of them up.

The problem is that it's difficult to wake people up and get them to turn against their tribe in an environment of such great political division. There is a deep cost to speaking up in the form of cancellation, but when you leave the left and speak up, you not only get canceled and smeared as a right-wing lunatic, you also lose your friends and possibly even your family.

As you're fighting back against the woke, please keep in mind that we can't just respond to the problem with aggression. There's a time and place for that, but there is also a time and place for ease and gentle conversations when people are ready. When I woke up, it didn't happen at the snap of a finger—it was a six-month process of exploration that followed a seed being planted in my head that something was very wrong. If I had been faced by a group of people calling me a "libtard" every day, this book probably would not exist because I would have never allowed myself to consider the idea that the other side wasn't as bad as they were being portrayed.

Following Biden's inauguration, the political right has grown angry, bitter, and mean. Not all of them, of course, but enough of them that it makes for a very difficult environment to wake people up into. In some respects, I understand it—they feel they had a presidency stolen; they lost the one person fighting for them (Donald Trump); they feel completely abandoned by their own leaders, many of their elected officials in the Republican Party are banned and censored on social media, and so on. There are a lot of reasons to be angry.

But my plea here is that we have got to keep our eyes on the bigger picture and serve the larger goal. We are in a cultural revolution. The desired outcome of the woke left is to slowly tear down our most important systems and institutions. They have a forty-year head start, and they are very good at what they are doing. We do not have much time left to beat this back.

What do you care about more: Owning the libs or winning the war? Pick one. You can't have both. If the priority is owning the libs, you'll get some temporary laughs and wake exactly zero people up because you haven't created a safe environment for them to land in. We must fight back smart. Otherwise, we'll be taking two steps back for every step forward.

If you're ready to win, let's keep going with some principles we can use to fight back.

# 11 Rules for the Actively Unwoke

I was once at an event with Christopher Rufo, a journalist who is the person leading the charge in the fight against Critical Race Theory. He said to me, "Everyone who is in this fight is separated by one degree from someone in this room." He was right. There were only a few dozen people there.

There are so few people fighting back because it is so hard. I wake up every single day questioning what dystopian nightmare I'll encounter today and wonder if there's a way I can be inserted back into the matrix. You will feel alone. You will feel helpless. You will feel overwhelmed.

The reason it's so hard is because the war against the woke is a battle of attrition. Whoever gives up first loses. You have to get up every day knowing it's hard now, but it will be harder if we lose. Exhausting us is one of their strategies—they simply yell and yell and yell and yell until you just give up and let them walk all over you to make it stop.

But it won't stop. This is a fight for the long haul, a fight for the big picture, for the values the union was founded on. And once you're in this fight, you're in it. Once you see what the woke are doing and what the big picture is, you can't unsee it. You either have to live with it every day, knowing it's there and trying your best to ignore it, or you do something about it.

That's a doom-and-gloom way to start a chapter so early in this book, but you have to know what you're getting into. Don't worry, I'll have a chapter on self-care when fighting the woke and what you need to know about getting canceled later in the book.

For now, you have to make the choice to join the unwoke army, or not. Hopefully if you've made it this far, you're in the game. In this chapter, I'll offer some general principles for fighting back that I believe can be applied in a variety of circumstances. In later chapters, I'll give you specific strategies that people have used to fight back in the real world.

## What We're Fighting For

The woke want a society in which the state hands out privileges on the basis of race. In order to effectively fight back, we have to present a different vision. It is not enough to simply be against the awful ideas of the woke. It is our job to be actively unwoke, with a more compelling vision of our own.

Our goal, at the highest level, is to create a society grounded in color indifference, individualism, and meritocracy.

- Color indifference is the idea the that we can see race and acknowledge that people of difference races may have a different experience in the world (based not only on their skin color but a variety of other factors, the most important of which is generally socioeconomic status). However, we fundamentally reject the idea that we should treat people differently based on the color of their skin. We are not blind to their race, as the term "colorblindness" suggests—we can see it. That doesn't mean we treat people differently because of it.

- Individualism is a natural follow-on to the idea of color indifference. If we are not going to treat people differently based on the color of their skin, then we must do a very controversial thing and focus instead on the content of people's character. (Oh, the horror!) Every human being has inherent value, and their immutable characteristics are most often the least interesting thing about them.
- Meritocracy reinforces that equality of opportunity is the goal, not equality of outcomes. We still have work to do to make sure that every person—regardless of their race or any other characteristic—has equal access to opportunity. However, our job is to make sure they have a chance to show up and do the work, not show up and get handed an outcome.

Long-term, winning looks like gaining back control of leadership positions in our major institutions from people who do not align with these core values. This is not about installing conservatives, Republicans, or anyone of any particular political persuasion. If you believe in the fundamental American values outlined in our Constitution, welcome aboard. We must be able to live in a place where we can disagree on some issues while still maintaining a commitment to a color-indifferent society grounded in individualism and meritocracy.

But we also need to face facts and know that we will not achieve that long-term goal anytime soon. Our immediate goal is much simpler than that: we have to slow them down.

Think of a fire hydrant pouring water onto the street. The water comes out so fast that it's impossible to stop it until the hydrant is closed, which you can only do with one of those big wrench tools that takes several large, beefy firefighters. You can't put your hands over it and stop it. You can't cover it with a piece of wood or anything else to stop the water—it's too powerful and will quickly get overwhelmed. The water is coming out at an unmanageable speed, quickly filling up the street until everyone is ankle deep.

This is the battle we're fighting with the woke every day. Ever since George Floyd's death, things have accelerated. Every single day there are dozens of new stories of new people, new schools, new businesses, new anti-racist trainers, new books, and new declarations of racism. Every single day more people are called out, and more things are labeled racist that weren't racist the day before.

Right now, our main goal has to be to shut the hydrant off, or at least screw it closed enough where we only have a trickle of water, not a constant, gushing stream.

The king woke warrior himself, James Lindsay, calls this throwing sand in their gears. He tells a story of being in college and there being a crazy guy on the street who would evangelize on his campus. So every day, James would go up and talk to him. While he was talking to him, he wasn't annoying everyone else around them! Every single day when he went up and talked to him, he was distracting him from annoying other people. He was throwing sand in his gears.

Our immediate goal is to get in their way and cause them enough trouble that it wastes their time, distracts them, or slows them down, even if it's just a little bit. Don't underestimate the pain we can cause them with what might seem like minor blows. And sometimes those things we think are going to be minor blows actually end up being much more impactful than we might dream.

If the only thing you can do right now is to slow them down, even if it's just for a moment, you must consider that a win and celebrate when you have successes. It's those celebrations that will keep getting you out of bed the next day.

## Rules for the Unwoke

Saul Alinsky has his *Rules for Radicals.* That's the woke playbook, the very thing they are still implementing today. If you haven't read it, you need to. For simplicity's sake, here are his top-level rules:

1. Power is not only what you have but what the enemy thinks you have.
2. Never go outside the experience of your people.
3. Wherever possible, go outside the experience of the enemy.
4. Make the enemy live up to their own book of rules.
5. Ridicule is man's most potent weapon.
6. A good tactic is one that your people enjoy.
7. A tactic that drags on too long becomes a drag.
8. Keep the pressure on.

9. The threat is usually more terrifying than the thing itself.
10. The major premise for tactics is the development of operations that will maintain a constant pressure upon the opposite.
11. If you push a negative hard and deep enough it will break through into its counterside.
12. The price of a successful attack is a constructive alternative.
13. Pick the target, freeze it, personalize it, and polarize it.

The most chilling part of Alinsky's book is an early chapter titled "Of Means and Ends." He describes the lengths they will go to in order to win, outlining how the winner will write the history books and will be able to massage whatever dirty tactics might be used to achieve the victory.

Just take a moment to wrap your head around that: decades ago, the woke told us they would do *anything* to win and then rewrite history to make themselves look like the good guys.

In order to combat that, we cannot pull punches. We cannot play nice. We cannot be afraid of engaging in conflict. We cannot be afraid of being called a racist. We are facing an enemy that has no ethics, no convictions, and is openly telling us they will lie, cheat, and steal in order to win.

Do you want these people to be the ones running the country?

In order to be actively unwoke, we have to develop our own rules. Because you don't fix things that aren't broken, some of the rules overlap with Alinsky's—they haven't been successful for no reason! However, oftentimes when we engage with his rules, it will be for different reasons than the radicals. Those are important distinctions to understand because they reflect our guiding values.

That's also the reason some of our rules will differ. Sometimes to be effective in this little game we're playing, we might need to be more aggressive than we want to be or than what we're used to, because that's what is necessary. However, you still have to stand for something. That's why we'll start at values.

## Rule #1: Know Your Values

Friedrich Nietzsche said, "*Beware that, when fighting monsters, you yourself do not become a monster...for when you gaze long into the abyss, the abyss gazes also into you.*"

Actually, there are at least a dozen slightly different versions of this quote floating around, but the point remains the same: when are you fighting evil, be careful that you yourself don't take on the qualities of the evil you're fighting. Sometimes we have to dabble in their squalor, but that doesn't mean we have to become them. That would defeat the entire purpose.

In the early part of my journey in the land of the politically homeless, I gravitated towards the Make America Great Again (MAGA) movement and eventually ended up doing something I never thought I would do in my life: I ended up supporting Donald Trump for reelection. The clincher for me was when he banned Critical Race Theory via executive order from all federal agencies and contractors—he was the only person to take action against it at that large of a scale. It was our first truly grand victory. (Not only has Joe Biden since rescinded those executive orders, but he's also actively working to integrate Critical Race Theory in every part of the federal bureaucracy, including cementing it in schools through the Department of Education.)

It's important to say here that I don't particularly care if you supported Donald Trump or not, if you think he really won or he didn't. None of those things matter anymore, and we have to come together to fight the greater menace. Bickering over which presidential candidate a person supported only allows the woke to win and distracts everyone from the larger fight.

However, I have to say something that will annoy the Trump-haters out there: the MAGA movement during the 2020 election was one of the most amazing, positive experiences of my life. There was so much love; I've never experienced anything like it. I'm not talking about the politicians—I'm talking about the average people, the voters. This group of people who had been characterized as horrible, evil, racists and white supremacists turned out to be some of the nicest people in the world.

After the election, and especially after January 6, things began to change. And after the inauguration of Joe Biden, I watched as so many people on the political right slowly turned into the monsters they were fighting. They started to become so reactionary to anything the left did (especially their most hated politician, Alexandria Ocasio-Cortez [AOC]) that it became completely distracting from the larger picture.

One of the most pronounced incidents came when there was a concerted effort to cancel Chrissy Teigen. Now, I'm not a Teigen fan by any stretch. However, all of a sudden there was a massive campaign led by some of the most well-known influencers on the right for tweets she had sent years before. Now granted, her tweets were absolutely bullying. And it wasn't the only time she had behaved badly. But no matter how you paint it, going after her two years after the fact wasn't for the principle. It was for revenge. And even worse, if you spoke up against it, you were attacked—a classic Social Justice Warrior (SJW) tactic to suppress dissent—so most people who disagreed with it just kept quiet.

Now, this is not to say the entire right has become the monster they're fighting—they haven't. But a portion of them have, and it has only hurt the greater picture. Sadly, the conservative influencers (typically the ones with a blue check on Twitter) have a more vested interest in making their audience angry than they do in fixing the problem.

We have to be better than them. We have to keep our eyes on the prize, because every time we allow ourselves to be distracted by petty battles like complaining about Jill Biden being called "Dr. Biden" or complaining about the latest lie AOC has told, the woke use it as a chance to make progress, and we've just lost ground.

Even when you have to fight, even when you have to get aggressive, even when you have to use their own tactics against them, you also have to be able to look yourself in the mirror at the end of the day and know that you did it for a reason: you achieved some positive movement, even if it's just a sliver of an inch.

We're fighting to protect freedom of speech for everyone, not just for the people we agree with.

We're fighting to make sure that everyone can participate in the discussion and that dissent is permitted without cancellation.

We're fighting for a true marketplace of ideas, one that utilizes debate instead of censorship and intimidation.

We're fighting for children to be able to go to school and learn HOW to think, not WHAT to think.

We've fighting because every time a child is told they can't achieve success in the world because of the color of their skin, that is child abuse. And it's happening in your local public school every day.

We're fighting for people to be able to support whatever political party they like without risking their job.

We're fighting to make sure people have the freedom to think and consider different ideas, and can even retain the right to change their mind based on new information.

We're fighting for a society in which we can celebrate all of the progress we've made over the last 250-plus years, while still acknowledging that things aren't perfect and there are still areas for improvement without being forced to say the country is foundationally racist.

We're fighting for the things the American Civil Liberties Union (ACLU) used to fight for—the most deplorable speech to still be protected, because when you protect the worst of the worst, you protect free speech for everyone else. And really, offensive speech is the only kind of speech that needs protection anyway. No one is going to demand cancellation for people they agree with.

Whatever you're fighting for, make sure you have a really clear picture of it in your head and hold yourself accountable to those values.

Take a few moments before you move on and write a few notes about why this fight is important to you. Every time the going gets rough, go back to your "why." Remind yourself why your "why" is important. And make sure you're holding yourself accountable to these values. There's so much noise out there—do not allow the nonsense to distract you by keeping your values and your "why" top of mind.

## Rule #2: Enjoy the Fight

I'm going to be honest: I don't know if we can win this fight. I really don't. But I do know that I'm not going to go down without fighting every step of the way.

People are split into two groups when it comes to engaging in conflict. Roughly 50 percent of people genuinely enjoy a good challenge and love the uphill journey of fighting back against an enemy. The other 50 percent want to dive under the table and hide anytime conflict rears its head.

In order to effectively fight back against the woke, you need to enjoy the conflict. It is impossible to be effective in this fight unless you are willing to piss people off. Every single time you piss someone off, you know you've moved the needle (or else they wouldn't be pissed off).

Remember in the previous chapter we discussed the success mindset, and one of the critical components of a success mindset is positive engagement, which means that you look at stress as an opportunity rather than something to be feared. This is simply a matter of perspective. We can always make the choice to look at things that happen to us with the worst possible interpretation or the best possible interpretation.

Let's say you go to a school board meeting and speak up against integrating Black Lives Matter into your kid's school curriculum. When you do it, you piss off a group of Karen moms who excommunicate your kid from the community play group because they don't want their child playing LEGOs with a child of racists. (Yes, this is a real possibility.)

Some might look at this as a bad thing—you lost a play group. But you can also look at it as a blessing. You just exposed the Karens for their true Karen nature. Maybe you thought they were normal people before, and now you know they're pod people. You know they're not your allies, and you can move on to find allies who will help the fight. Remember, there are more people on your team than there are on theirs. You've just identified a bunch of people who are not on your team. That opens the door for new people who are on your team to come into your life.

You always have the power to change your perspective, and the more you're able to do it, the more energy you'll have for the fight that really matters. When you piss people off, instead of being afraid that you're going to be canceled, revel in the fact that you got their goat enough that you set them off. Let their anger fuel your commitment. Know that you only start taking flack when you are over the target. Tell yourself whatever you need to in order for you to truly believe that this is a good thing.

If you want bonus points, start looking at it as a game. In video games, you have to go through a series of progressively harder challenges until you meet the final boss and free the princess (or whatever it is). Look at fighting the woke as the same type of game. Regardless of whether you're fighting back by building awareness, going after the schools, speaking up in the workplace, creating art to try to influence culture, make it FUN. Try to gamify the fight. Create positive incentives for your wins. Reframe everything in terms of making the fight a fun experience so you can trick your brain into enjoying the fight.

You are fighting for something noble, an ideal that has lit the world's beacon of hope for almost 250 years. Yes, it's hard. Yes, it can be exhausting. Yes, it seems as though we are in an unwinnable fight. But while we're in it, we might as well make the most of it.

When the founders of the United States declared independence from their British overlords, they committed treason. If we had lost that fight, the founders would have been executed. They fought for purpose, for what they knew was correct. The fight we are in today is to extend the legacy they started in 1776 (not in 1619). Show up and celebrate that you're a part of keeping their great experiment alive.

## Rule #3: Stop Accepting Their Rules

If the Devil came up from hell and said, "We're going to play a game. If I win, you spend an eternity with me in fire and brimstone. If you win, you get to spend eternity in a beautiful, cushy mansion on a cloud with God. The rules of the game are that I get to set all the rules and can change them anytime, for any reason."

Does that sound fair? Does that sound like a set of terms you should accept without questioning it?

Accepting terms like that without question is the most common mistake people make in fighting back against the woke.

For example, the woke believe everyone who is born white is a racist. Oftentimes, I'll see people reference this fact as though it's an accepted truth instead of something the woke just made up to use to their advantage.

If someone calls you a racist, here's what you say: "No, I'm not."

When you do that, you can expect the woke to trot out their redefined definition of racism—that it's prejudice plus power. They also might say that you're upholding white supremacy because of systemic racism.

If someone does that, here's what you say: "I don't agree with any of that."

It's that simple. Don't elaborate. (You don't owe them that.) Don't be defensive. (You're allowed to see the world in a different way.) Just state clearly and assertively that you disagree with the entire premise of their argument.

Make no mistake, they're not going to like it. They will probably encourage you to find your nearest gulag and report for reeducation camp immediately (or minimally tell you that you need to educate yourself). But you are under no obligation to acknowledge the validity of their perspective. No matter how much they try to guilt you or gaslight you, stand your ground.

The woke have been the ones proactively fighting this battle for decades, while the rest of us have been reacting to it. That means that oftentimes, we find ourselves on the back foot. Because we're reacting, it can be easy to overlook the premise of the argument. But you must always remember that the woke are entirely making this shit up. It's disillusion. Fantasy. You can accept their premise if you choose to, but they are not entitled to it.

Not accepting their premise exploits one of their worst fears—losing control. Remember how we discussed the personality type of the woke tending more towards the Dominant and Conscientious side of the DISC model? What those styles hate more than almost anything else is losing control. That is their kryptonite. When you use this as your weapon, they get angry and then they start making mistakes. That's when you can go in for the kill.

## Rule #4: Come at Them, Bro!

I once debated Critical Race Theory on YouTube teamed with Gothix and Christian Watson (both people you should follow and subscribe to if you're interested in these topics) against two CRT academics, who shall remain nameless to protect the guilty. I knew that the conversation would likely revolve around them making a convoluted argument that we didn't know what the definition of Critical Race Theory was. They would rely on obscure academic sources they pulled out of their back pocket for the specific purpose of confusing people.

So I did the only sensible thing and hit them right between the eyes with an opening statement declaring in very assertive terms that I did not care about CRT from an academic perspective, nor did I care about any of their obscure journal articles. I only cared how CRT manifested itself in the real world in regard to trainings in the workplace or classroom instruction in schools. I was unwilling to engage in any discussion that didn't focus on how the average person experiences Critical Race Theory.

This aggressive approach pissed them off so badly that the two experts who were working on their PhDs on the topic found themselves completely unable to produce a definition of Critical Race Theory during the first ninety minutes of the debate. Of course, they clutched their pearls that I would do such a thing as dismiss their argument without considering it and that I didn't act as though I were participating in the collegiate debate they were apparently expecting. They continued to mock me after the debate—how DARE I dismiss their scholarly work!

And that's how I knew I got them. I treated them with the righteous indignation they rightfully deserved, and it broke their ability to mount an argument in front of a live audience. The fact that they were kicking and screaming after the fact just emphasized the win.

The woke do not know how to handle it when you come at them. They are so used to being the aggressors that when someone else assumes that role, it throws them off balance in a way that is difficult for them to come back from. Doing so harkens back to rule #3—you're taking them out of control.

The majority of people reading this will likely not feel comfortable with that level of assertiveness. But the reality is that just because it's not your natural tendency to be that assertive in regular life, just because you feel uncomfortable, doesn't mean you can't do it. It just means you need a bit of practice to become more comfortable. Think of yourself as acting in a play—you're not performing as yourself. You're being the person you need to be for that particular situation in order to be the most effective.

One caveat to this rule is that you have to be mindful about where you are implementing it. For example, if you're required to go to a diversity training in your workplace (the thing that pays your mortgage), getting up and reading the trainer the riot act is probably not going to work out well for you. However, if you're at a school board meeting ready to give your kid's principal a piece of your mind, let it rip.

In October 2020, a woman no one had ever heard of posted a video to YouTube titled, "Dear Smith College: I Have a Few Requests."

> Hi, my name's Jodi Shaw. I work at Smith College. I've worked there for the past three years. Right now, I work as an admin assistant (it's called student support coordinator) in the Department of Res Life and Division of Student Affairs. I also graduated from Smith College, so I'm an alum. And I'm white...and that really shouldn't be relevant, but my employer has made it clear over and over and over again that not only is it relevant, but it's possibly one of the most important, if not THE most important, feature of me as a human.

After speaking off the record with a number of staff members at the college, Jodi choose to take the bold action of publicly making the following requests of her employer:

- Stop reducing her personhood to a racial category.
- Stop telling her how she should feel about herself because of her race.
- Stop presuming to know who she is or what her culture is based on her skin color.
- Stop asking her to project racial stereotypes and assumptions onto others based on their skin color.

- Stop telling her young women of color have no power and agency in the world.
- Stop telling her that young white women have power and privilege over everyone else.
- Stop demanding she admit she has white privilege and work on her implicit bias as a condition of her continued employment.
- Stop telling her that as a white person, she is especially responsible for dismantling systemic racism.
- Stop enabling students to act abusively to staff by refusing to hold them accountable for their own behavior.

Lastly, she stated that all Smith College employees have the right to work in an environment free of the ever-present terror that any unverified student allegation of racism has the power to crush their reputations, ruin their livelihoods, or endanger the physical safety of themselves or their family members.

As thanks for her efforts, Jodi was placed on administrative leave pending an investigation before eventually resigning her position a few months later.

Don't worry, there's a silver lining: Instead of accepting a lucrative settlement offered by the college that would require her to keep quiet, Jodi chose to continue to fight, opting to sue Smith College for creating a hostile work environment. Inspired by her efforts, online supporters helped her raise over $300,000 (as of this writing) to provide her with the security net she lost when she refused the settlement.

But she doesn't plan to keep it all for herself—she plans to start an organization to help others who have found themselves in a similar position.

Jodi committed what is simultaneously the single most simple, complex, and important act in the war against the woke: she spoke up and told the truth.

Telling the truth seems so easy, doesn't it? It's one of the first things children learn and is so basic to our societal moral code that it's in the Ten Commandments. Yet, when push comes to shove, the lack of individuals standing up and telling the truth about their disagreement with the woke ideology is one of the biggest challenges in fighting back.

We've already discussed how this is a battle of attrition—whoever gives up first loses. But the second, more important battle within the larger war is which side will present the most compelling argument. Strategically, this is just as important as outlasting the competition, because whoever speaks up the with the most vigor will ultimately win.

When you speak up, you inspire others to do the same. When Jodi Shaw told her story, she inspired Aaron Kindsvatter to follow in her footsteps. Aaron was a professor of counseling at the University of Vermont, a publicly-funded institution that was pulling the same crap that Jodi experienced at Smith. Aaron bravely told his story, which made the spotlight on the problem larger.

Imagine how big the spotlight would be if everyone at every university that was indoctrinating tuition-paying students into the woke ideology spoke up? It would be an unstoppable force.

## Rule #6: Mock Them Relentlessly

On Friday afternoons, I go live on my YouTube channel for a regular show I call *Happy Hour*. This is a stream that's designed to help my audience blow off steam at the end of the week by having a drink or two, watching a training based on Critical Race Theory, and mocking it relentlessly while also pointing out the flaws and hypocrisy rampant in these types of presentations.

Oh, who am I kidding—it blows off steam for me too! Watching woke trainings all day isn't exactly how I envisioned my career going.

It was during *Happy Hour* that I first encountered anti-racist educator Kate Slater. In one of the first streams I did, we watched her give a presentation called "4 Steps to Begin An Anti-Racist Education" for the University of New Hampshire. It was later archived on the university's website, where I came across it months after it had been given.

In that presentation, Kate outlined the responsibilities of a good white anti-racist ally with the four *s*'s:

- *Show up*, which seems to be defined as admitting that you have a problem. She's looking for her audience to show up with a statement like, "Hello, my name is John, and I am a racist white person."
- *Shut up and listen*, in which the now-admitted racist white ally is supposed to read a series of books and articles by black authors and anti-racist trainers designed to outline everything that is wrong with whiteness. The ally is not permitted to ask questions about any of the content—dissent is only proof that step one was not achieved properly and that the ally is still denying their obvious racism.
- *Support*, which is framed as providing support for people of color unquestioningly but is more about

supporting the anti-racist movement than it is about supporting individuals.

- *School yourself*, which is about constantly reminding yourself that, as a white person, you are a racist.

This is what was taught in a training given at a public university supported by taxpayer dollars. As of this writing, it is still available to watch on the University of New Hampshire's website.

The next time Kate showed up in a training for *Happy Hour* it was for a similar webinar given by a different professor at the University of New Hampshire who was using his platform at a state-funded institution to advocate against a proposed law that would limit the teaching of Critical Race Theory in the state. She popped in for a cameo to oppose a law that would not allow her to earn taxpayer money for trainings in which she told people to "shut up and listen" purely on the basis of their race.

And so it continued like this. I would watch these trainings every Friday, and Kate would sometimes have surprise cameos. I'd say, "Isn't she that crazy lady from the University of New Hampshire?", we'd make fun of her, I'd lament that she was benefitting from my taxes to spread her nonsense, and life would go on.

I knew we had a future wannabe Robin DiAngelo (a.k.a. white lady savior) on our hands, but I didn't know exactly what to do about it since Kate wasn't saying anything that was substantially different than every other anti-racist trainer I had observed. But sometimes, when you're fighting the woke, it is just about waiting for the right opportunity to present itself.

Then, the big one happened. Kate happened to find herself in a discussion in which she and two other anti-racist educators ganged up on a progressive white male teacher named Will Reusch in an attempt to browbeat him into agreeing that Critical Race Theory belonged in K-12 schools. At one point, they compared Critical Race Theory to a religion (hint: it is one), and one of the protagonists actually argued that the Constitution should be burned as a solution for systemic racism.

The two-hour conversation was held live on Instagram, and the recording of it spread like wildfire in the unwoke community, purely because of how painful it was to watch. After I watched on my *Happy Hour* stream, I immediately decided that Kate had shown up enough by accident on my channel that it was time for me to make contact.

I sent her a note on Instagram asking her if she would come on and debate her ideas with me.

She promptly declined.

Not one to give up easily, I made a video and put it on my Instagram challenging Kate publicly. After all, I argued, if she declined an invitation for a discussion that would just be proof of her obvious white fragility, and we wouldn't want that. I was giving her the opportunity to do the work and have an uncomfortable conversation.

After that, my followers started popping over to Kate's profile to tell her explicitly what they thought of her idea that they should "shut up."

All it took was a little public pressure to make magic happen. After blocking anyone who dared to post a comment on one of her photos, Kate posted the following statement:

A few points of clarification:

1. "Debates" about Critical Race Theory are often straw men for debates about whether or not systemic racism is real. And no number of statistics or facts that I could offer up are going to convince people to "see" systemic racism if they don't want to.
2. Yes, all white people are racist in that all white people have been conditioned in a society where one's racial identity determines life experiences / outcomes and whiteness is the norm and the default. That includes me!
3. I don't hate white people—I hate whiteness. To distinguish between the two, please feel free to watch my recent live "What is whiteness?"
4. CRT does not create oppression: It names oppression that already exists.

Kate made a key mistake in this Instagram post: she overtly said she believes that "all white people are racist" and that she "hates whiteness." Mocking her work over the course of months and directly challenging her (à la rule #4) had forced her into the mistake of saying the quiet part out loud.

The woke can get away with saying almost anything, but when they are this direct about believing that racism is the sole property of white people and that all white people are guilty regardless of their thoughts or behaviors, that generally lands them in very hot water. It's the thing that is the easiest for the average person to identify as being complete and utter nonsense. Even if they know nothing about Critical Race Theory or about the havoc that the woke have wreaked, they can look at a statement like "all white people are racist" and think, "Wait a minute...that's not right."

Kate made the extra mistake of declaring that all white people are racist in the context of having recently accepted a job at the VERY white Brandeis University as the assistant dean of student affairs. How can she effectively serve a predominantly white student body if she believes all of those students to be racist?

Being actively unwoke means that you jump on opportunities for the mockery of true believers and use them for everything they are worth to show the world what the woke really think and how they operate.

I seized on it immediately, grabbed a screenshot of her statement, and started posting it on Twitter and Instagram asking why Brandeis would employ an admitted racist. Because I have a reasonably large platform, that was all it took. People then took my screenshot and started sharing it with their audiences, bewildered at why a young white woman would say that she was a racist because of how she was born.

Over the next few days, Kate's statements were featured on Fox News, the *New York Post*, *Newsweek*, the *Toronto Sun*, and were plastered on the home page of the *Daily Mail* in the UK.

In response, she took her Twitter account completely offline and made her Instagram account private. Kate Slater had been overtly exposed to the world, and these articles and images will come up anytime someone searches for her name. Millions of people were exposed to a previously unknown anti-racist educator arguing that all white people are racist. And, for a brief moment, her personal reach and influence with her teachings became more limited.

There are few things the woke hate more than having their ideas challenged, questioned, or mocked, which is why they almost never debate in an open setting. But when you engage strategies like this, you can force them into making a mistake.

That's your goal: Get them to say the most direct thing you can, screenshot it (they may delete it later), and then expose it. Get as many eyes on it as possible and explain clearly and concisely what it means—"An Assistant Dean of Students at a major university believes white people are racist," accompanied by clear evidence.

It might seem as though the only goal to this type of strategy is humiliation of the target. I'll admit, that's a nice bonus. Although I don't typically take joy in watching people be humiliated, you must keep it in context: anti-racist trainers make a career out of humiliating people.

However, that's not the goal. The goal is to slow them down while exposing the hypocrisy to the masses. This is what throwing sand in their gears looks like.

## Rule #7: Blow the Whistle

The example of Kate in rule #6 wasn't just about mockery. It was about exposure. The more daylight we can shine on what the woke are doing at all different levels the better, particularly when they are overtly telling us how crazy their ideas are.

If your organization or school is promoting woke ideas, document everything. Save presentations, record webinars, take as many photos and screenshots as you can without getting caught, and make that information public. People want to hear your story, and exposing the woke's own materials has been one of the most effective ways of fighting back.

Christopher Rufo is the general in the battle against the woke because he releases companies' primary source documentation sent to him by whistleblowers, everything from Raytheon to Lockheed Martin to Disney. His work almost single-handedly changed the narrative surrounding Critical Race Theory, resulting in Trump's original executive orders and legislation across the country.

People make the mistake of thinking you need thousands of followers to make a difference or that you need to expose your identity and put your job or social standing at risk—you don't. And if you've got something really juicy and need help exposing it to the masses, get in touch with people like me, James Lindsay, Chris Rufo, or any other unwoke influencer, and we can help you spread the word or boost your exposure. Believe me, we want to hear from you. It's the job of all of us to expose this nonsense for what it is. Regardless of whether you have two followers or two million, we are all on the same team.

## Rule #8: Never Bend the Knee, No Matter What

Dan Richards is a successful entrepreneur in New Hampshire who committed the crime of wanting to donate an entrepreneurship program to his son's high school and attended a PTA meeting held via Zoom one evening to discuss the idea. Well, he happened to attend on a night when they were talking about diversity training. Dan had a previous interaction with the school's principal about Critical Race Theory and even completed an assigned set of readings designed to "educate" him (as a white man) on the topic. Sadly, the readings had the opposite effect than was intended—they convinced Dan that all of this was a bunch of nonsense, and he rejected the premise of it entirely. When the moms on the PTA began discussing their equity plan, Dan interjected that he didn't think this was a good idea.

Thus the struggle session began. The moms in the meeting formed their angry mob and began coming for Dan demanding he repent his impertinence, all live on the internet for anyone to witness. Apparently, it got so bad that people started texting Dan's wife (who was in the other room) asking if things were OK. She replied that Dan was at a PTA meeting, why wouldn't it be OK?

But Dan never backed down. In fact, this attack strengthened his resolve that something was rotten in Denmark, and he became one of the strongest unwoke allies in the state of New Hampshire, playing a pivotal role in waging the battle against Critical Race Theory at the state level.

Rule #8 is probably the most important thing about fighting back against the woke—once you start the fight, you must stand your ground and never give in. Never bend the knee EVER. Do not give them one single inch, because as soon as you do, they will take a mile.

We've talked about how this is a war of attrition on a large scale, but every single battle within it is also based on attrition. When you speak up and fight back against them, their only goal is to make you give up and retreat. They will lie, cheat, and overtly gaslight you in order to achieve their goals. You must remember that you are not having a conversation with a reasonable person—you are having a conversation with a person whose only goal is to get you to shut up. The minute you give in is the minute they know they've gained power over you. The demands will never stop. Once they get you the first time, they know they'll be able to get you again and again.

When you stand your ground and say "NO," you can also accomplish another important goal—you begin to make their tactics socially unacceptable by threatening them with the righteous indignation they deserve. One of the reasons the woke have been so successful is because they use the psychological tactic of social ostracization—when you believe you're going to lose your job, your reputation, your friends, and your family due to cancellation and public shaming, it is a lot easier to give up and go along with what they want than it is to persist.

We need to turn the tables back on them—make their tactics socially unacceptable by simply refusing to engage. Keep in mind that every time you stand your ground and show courage in the face of adversity, you demonstrate what it looks like to others, and you can give them the courage to do the same.

## Rule #9: Build Social Support

Alinsky's thirteenth rule for radicals is "pick the target, freeze it, personalize it, and polarize it."

That's what the woke are doing every single time they cancel someone—they are trying to isolate the target to make them feel as though they are alone and helpless in the world, that they will never achieve social acceptance.

The only way to combat that is to have some method of social support in place. That could come from your friends and your family. It could come from building a network of individuals who are as dedicated to fighting back against this menace as you are. Or it could come from a combination of the two. (That's probably the safest option because, as much as I hate to say it, it's not out of the realm of possibility that you could lose your friends and family as a result of this fight.)

The good news is that the numbers are on our side. In June 2020, YouGov released poll results stating that 58 percent of Americans who believe they understand what Critical Race Theory is do not have a good impression of it. Only 38 percent of those who say they understand it support it. That means the odds are in your favor, but also allow it to give you the confidence to take the first step.

Included in this rule is the idea that we shouldn't be turning people away from the fight unless there is a very good reason for it. I watch influencers make this mistake all the time, particularly among the intellectuals who love to intellectualize about the problem who want to exclude anyone who associated themselves with the MAGA movement or (God forbid!) who voted for Donald Trump in 2020. There is also a fair bit of infighting within the anti-woke community. (Admittedly, I've engaged in some of it myself, but only when someone else "punched" me first, and I was defending myself.)

We have to stop with all of this nonsense, and if you haven't engaged with it yet, make the commitment not to. The only thing that should matter is beating back the existential crisis. I don't need to like you or want to be best friends in order to support anything you'd contribute to winning the war, and no one else should be putting conditions on it either. We have a bigger enemy than we can handle already. Every second you spend fighting back against your own team, you are allowing them to win. You can't control anyone else's behavior, and I absolutely believe you should stand up for yourself if attacked, but you can control what you're giving. Just don't start nonsense unless it absolutely needs to be started.

Being actively unwoke is a heavy burden to bear when you are on your own. The good news is that you don't have to be. Never forget that we have numbers on our side, we just need to build spaces for them to connect. Look for every opportunity you can to create groups of like-minded people to go into battle together. Talk to each other. Support each other. Have each other's back. We need you all for the long haul.

## Rule #10: Not All Battles Are Created Equal

When you put yourself in a position of engaging with war, it can become very easy to see everything as a battle worthy of your energy. But the reality is that not all battles are worth fighting, and to win a war of attrition that probably will not be won in any of our lifetimes, we need to make sure we're focusing our energy wisely.

In order to do that, we have to take a nuanced look at the situation, acknowledging that different contexts call for different strategies. For instance, you probably wouldn't fight back in your workplace the same way you would in your kid's school, or the same way you would if you were engaging the woke on Twitter, or if you had a podcast, and so on and so forth. Although there is certainly some overlap of our rules across these different arenas, there are also simple truths we must acknowledge: if you can't pay your mortgage, you're going to be far less likely effective in giving that kick-ass speech at the school board meeting, so you want to make sure you're putting your energies where they matter. To give yourself the gift of that security, don't do something that's likely to get you fired from your job out of nowhere.

Through the next several chapters, we'll discuss the nuances at play and how I recommend navigating them. For right now, I just need you to acknowledge that they exist and being a bull in a china shop simply isn't the best strategy for every situation. Fighting back means fighting strategically where you can get the most gain for your efforts.

## Rule #11: Wake People Up

Many of our rules for the actively unwoke revolve around going into battle. That's why I think it's important to end on moving towards peace. When you're living in a war zone, sometimes it can be difficult to remember that our goal is not to live in perpetual war.

Our goal is to find peace. A peace in which we will experience a color-indifferent society grounded in individualism and meritocracy.

The only way we will find peace is by waking people up. That is the ball game. That is why we must prioritize opportunities to wake people up above all else.

I'm going to be honest: the political right really drops the ball in this case. And it's extraordinarily disappointing because I want them to be better at this, and I feel like I can envision a future reality where they are, but they are so horrible at taking advantage of opportunities, it's absurd.

Let me give you one example: Caitlyn Jenner's campaign for governor of California during the effort to recall Gavin Newsom. Full disclosure: this book is being written prior to the recall election but will be published after it, so I don't know what happened. Thankfully, it's not the point of the anecdote.

The point is that the right will take advantage of every opportunity to shoot themselves in the foot. When I heard about Caitlyn Jenner's run, my first reaction was to think, "What an amazing opportunity to red pill people who won't know how to handle the Republicans supporting a trans woman while the Democrats support a white man!" Let's be honest, California is basically a lost cause anyway, so you might as well use it as an opportunity to strike a blow in the culture war. Also, Caitlyn was always a conservative! I didn't understand how they could possibly screw this up.

But they did. She was denounced almost immediately by the blue-check influencers. People went out of their way to call her by her former name and purposefully misgender her. The political right behaved precisely how the political left expected them to behave. They didn't just say, "Nah, not our cup of tea." They came out with aggressive fury at the mere notion that a trans woman would dare throw their name in a hat. They behaved towards Caitlyn Jenner the way the political left behaves towards Trump.

And so, a rare opportunity was lost to red pill millions by presenting a different image of the Republican Party than had been told in the corporate media. And it was lost for no good reason, other than Republicans cared more about getting their digs in than they did about winning. They didn't have to like her. Literally all they had to do was not be raging assholes. That's it.

We've got to be smarter about this. No matter how much you get off on fighting, if all we do is fight all day every day, we are no better than the woke enemy we're fighting.

Most opportunities to wake people up come in the form of one-on-one or small group conversations that start by planting a seed that something is wrong. When you have the opportunity to have these conversations, don't go in like you're jumping into battle. You'll just come across too aggressively. This is not a YouTube debate, a Twitter spat, or a school board meeting—this is a private conversation where you're asking someone else to be vulnerable. I speak from experience when I say that it is an extremely jarring, anxiety-producing journey to wake up and realize everything you've believed for most of your life is wrong. You already feel like you're going crazy. The last thing you need in that moment is someone getting right in your face demanding you apologize for every time you were wrong.

Have the important conversations gently. And for the love of God, don't screw up the big opportunities.

## Let's Keep Going

We've got our eleven rules for the actively unwoke. Now, let's look at how we can apply these rules in some specific situations of our primary battlegrounds: the schools, corporate America, the government, and culture.

# PART 2

## Field Guide for Fighting Back

# Indoctrination Factories

Imagine sending your biracial son off to school thinking he would learn fundamentals like reading, writing, math, and the like—only to discover that his school was teaching him that he's an oppressor because his skin color was light enough to be deemed "white-passing."

This is precisely what happened to Gabrielle Clark and her son, William Clark.

When William was a high school senior, he was required to take a course titled "Sociology of Change" in order to graduate from Democracy Prep at the Agassi Campus charter school in Las Vegas. In this class, students were required to publicly reveal their race, gender identity, religion, and sexual orientation and then assign labels such as "oppressor" or "oppressed" to each identity to discover how much privilege they have. If students were deemed to be oppressors based on their identity, they were asked to unlearn the beliefs, attitudes, and behaviors that come with being privileged.

The slides from the course (which you can view at activelyunwoke.com/clarkcase) also insinuated that racism against white people is impossible because racism is defined as "prejudice + power," their updated definition of racism based on the oppression hierarchy that we've previously discussed.

The slides also asserted that traditional family structure and religion reenforce homophobic prejudices, that government (the police especially) promotes stereotypes and prejudices, that people who are deemed "oppressed" have internalized inferiority, and that people who are white have an unearned sense of entitlement and have accepted "oppressed" people as inherently inferior.

William, having a good head on his shoulders from being raised by a very strong mother, objected to being forced to say he was an oppressor in order to receive a passing grade. Gabrielle supported this decision and contacted the school to request William be excused from the class. Not only was that request denied, but the school retaliated against them, putting William's graduation at risk.

In this situation, most parents would have put their head down and asked their child to do what the teacher asks, even if they don't agree with it. Get the passing grade and get the heck out of the school.

But remember, when it comes to dealing with the woke, bending the knee is always the wrong answer. Every single time you bend the knee to their absurd requests just to have it over and done with, you just give them more power and open yourself up to all future attacks.

Gabrielle is one hell of a fighter. She contacted me with screenshots of the slides that had been used in William's class, as well as the letter from the principle denying her request to remove him from the class. I made a video of it and posted it on my YouTube channel to give her case more exposure. I even learned later that school officials had pondered hiring some public relations help in response to the video! Anytime they're hiring a PR firm, you know you've put them on their heels.

The coverage of her situation gave Gabrielle an internal boost—sometimes when we have people fighting for us, that gives us the courage to keep on fighting ourselves. She kept going, eventually connecting with a lawyer named Jon O'Brien (schoolhouserights.com) who was brave enough to take on her case. Gabrielle sued the school, the very first lawsuit in the country against Critical Race Theory in schools. As of this writing, the case is still ongoing, and Gabrielle is committed to fighting until the very end. Her goal isn't to settle, but rather to set a legal precedent. Luckily, in the meantime, they did receive an injunction against the school that allowed William to graduate and move on with his life.

## The Teachers Are Not Your Friends

If there is one thing you must take away from this chapter it's that many (not all, but many) of the teachers in your children's schools are not your friends. They are not your partners. They see it as not just their job but as their moral obligation to insert themselves between parents and students.

- Teachers in Loudoun County, Virginia, organized a Facebook group to plot and plan against parents who objected to Critical Race Theory being taught in schools. They compiled a list of parents who disagreed with the practice and planned to infiltrate their groups, hack their websites, and expose their identity publicly. They even fundraised to support their efforts.

- When parents in one Missouri school district started questioning if their schools were teaching Critical Race Theory, teachers were advised by their higher-ups to create a fake curriculum to send home to parents so they would get out of their hair. They then continued to teach anti-racism in a curriculum only used in the classroom when the parents weren't looking.
- Teachers are openly discussing how much they detest it when parents red pill their children by offering a different perspective than what teachers give in the classroom and are signing pledges to say they will not enforce state-level laws banning the teaching of Critical Race Theory.

How bad is it?

Let's put it this way: Have you ever thought of homeschooling your children?

No, really. That's how bad it is. I promise you, the homeschooling industry is about to experience a major boom, so if you're invested in helping parents do that in any way, you'll probably do very well.

Our K-12 education system is completely compromised.

- The Arizona Department of Education utilizes a chart that says children begin to become racist at three years old.
- I've seen schools integrating Critical Race Theory into the curriculum as early as pre-kindergarten. That's teaching CRT to children starting at four years old.

- Lessons around social justice, equity, and anti-racism are being integrated ACROSS the curriculum. That means, most of the time, they are not going to appear as a stand-alone class like the one William Clark took. Rather, they will be taught as part of a course like history, English, sciences, drama, and even math. Yes, math is now racist.
- This is all happening at a time when the Nation's Report Card (https://www.nationsreportcard.gov/) is reporting that only 23 percent of eighth grade students at public schools are proficient in civics, 33 percent proficient in math, 32 percent proficient in reading, and only 26 percent are proficient in writing. Schools are no longer teaching the basics. They are teaching activism. At the same time, they are dumbing down your children enough so that they do not have the ability to question and challenge what they are being taught at the most basic level.

If your children are in public schools, they have likely been taught, or will be taught, by someone who has been trained in the art of woke. Please allow me to walk you through a visualization exercise so that you might understand how bad this problem is:

- The vast majority of current teachers in public schools today have had at least one anti-racist training based in Critical Race Theory, whether it was voluntary or mandatory.
- A very large percentage of that first group who has taken at least one training has taken more than one

training. Many of them consider it a moral obligation to "do the work" to counteract their inherent racism.
- Even more terrifying, most of the teachers working today probably completed teacher education programs in which Critical Race Theory was integrated throughout their course of study. It was embedded and inescapable if they wanted to become teachers.
- And for those who encountered Critical Race Theory in college, a very large percent of them had professors who, themselves, were brought into the woke ideology in exactly the same way.

In other words, the problems we have in the public schools today are a generational problem. There is no quick solve to it. Even if we start right this second with all the muscle we have, it will still take a new generation of teachers and teacher educators/trainings to replace the sheer volume of teachers who have gone through programs that indoctrinated them to the woke mind virus. This is what happens when the woke get a forty-year head start—it leads to an unfixable problem.

And I hate to be the bearer of bad news, but the problem gets even worse: do not expect the state bans on Critical Race Theory in schools to save you. They are an interim blockade to a problem that will require real and significant culture change to reign back in.

Some context to help you understand the lay of the land: The battle against Critical Race Theory began to build steam in 2020 and into 2021, with more and more people becoming aware of the menace of CRT. Chris Rufo had continued his leadership in the fight against it in the media, breaking story after story and becoming the de facto public leader in the fight against CRT. I had broken one of the most high-profile CRT stories there was by exposing the Coca-Cola's "Be Less White" training to tens of millions of people (you'll hear about that in the next chapter), which generated a significant amount of awareness of the problem. Parents were being exposed to what their children were really being taught in the public schools after a full year of online education. Joe Biden had rescinded Donald Trump's executive orders banning CRT in all state agencies and contractors on day one of his presidency, so we were off to the races. As of this writing, twenty-two states had introduced legislation that would effectively ban state-funded CRT, including in schools.

And some of those bills started passing. Idaho, Oklahoma, Iowa, Tennessee, Texas, and even my home state of New Hampshire passed a version of it. In Florida, it was banned in schools by executive order from the governor.

All this is to say that there was more public awareness regarding the problem than ever, and people who had been previously unaware of the culture war did not like what they were seeing.

In response, the woke left started freaking out. They knew that we were onto their game, and they started doing what they always do in these situations: they doubled down. In the immortal words of author Vox Day, "SJWs always double down."

In May 2021, the website Chalkbeat published an article titled "'Teaching the truth': Tennessee educators respond to proposed limits on teaching about racism." It quoted an elementary school teacher who proudly proclaimed, "To be frank, the bill will not make it harder for my personal classroom because I plan to ignore it. Who's going to enforce it?"

In June 2021, a high school history teacher in Texas posted a video on TikTok explaining that she doesn't explicitly teach Critical Race Theory but that CRT, in practice, is woven into her entire US history classroom. She continued that she didn't believe you could teach US history responsibly without weaving in elements from CRT.

Also in June 2021, a high school history teacher in Colorado proudly tweeted, "I'm going on record now: At the end of the day it's just my students and me in our classroom and we will be discussing race, class and gender in my history classes, regardless of what laws or policies people want to pass. Critical race theory is a component of everything I do."

In every state that has "banned" Critical Race Theory from being taught in the classrooms, teachers have proudly proclaimed that they plan to ignore the laws entirely. The Zinn Education Project launched a petition signed by over five thousand teachers publicly pledging to break anti-CRT laws and teach the subject matter anyway.

And in July 2021, the National Education Association (NEA) convened an annual assembly that approved a resolution to promote CRT in all fifty states and over fourteen thousand school districts in which it collaborates with. They also approved a $56,000 spend on opposition research against opponents of CRT, like Chris Rufo.

The woke are not going to go down without a fight, and they will throw everything they have at us. While all the areas the woke have woven their tentacles into are important battlegrounds, government-funded public schools are the most important front for us to fight. Not only are they training teachers and staff in the ways of the woke, but they are also indoctrinating the most vulnerable into the ideology before their brains have fully developed the ability to think logically.

There was a time when students could make it all the way through high school without being exposed to this ideology and would only discover it in college. Sadly, because so few people fought back, the woke began moving the bar earlier and earlier until they ended up teaching CRT before they started teaching students to read. This is why you cannot just shut your eyes and say, "It'll go away if we just ignore it." The only job the woke have is to create more people who are woke, and they will not go away until it is made culturally unacceptable for them to continue.

If you can only fight back in one area, this is the battleground to choose. We will never win the war against the woke without dealing drastically with public, government-funded education. And get ready, because it might require severe and revolutionary overhaul.

## Be Actively Unwoke in Schools

Let's explore some practical ways we can fight back. If everyone with school-aged children did something to fight back, we'd be well on our way to winning in no time. Choose one thing to do, whichever one works the best for you. This list is ordered from what's generally the easiest to the most difficult task to complete—even if you just do the easiest thing, you'll still make a difference.

The important thing is not that you choose the biggest and most challenging task. It's not that you take on everything. It's not that you spend hours a day fighting back like crazy people like I do. The most important thing is that you take action.

Small action is still action. Once you master the small things, move on to the bigger ones.

*Pay attention to your kid's homework and know the words to watch out for.* One of the blessings of the pandemic was that, for the first time, parents got a clear view into precisely what their children were learning. That said, it can sometimes be a little bit tricky to identify if your kids are learning woke curriculum or not. Here are some key words to watch out for:

- Whiteness
- Privilege (based on race, gender, sexual orientation, religion, and the like)
- White Fragility
- Equity (especially if they are opposing it with equality)
- Systemic Racism
- Anti-racism/Anti-racist
- Safe Space
- Oppression/Oppressor/Oppressed
- Power + Privilege
- Social Justice

If any of these words or phrases show up, chances are they are learning things you don't want taught in public schools. For example, if your school has an equity committee, they are teaching Critical Race Theory whether they admit it or not.

For this exercise, it is critically important to understand that, in K-12 schools, they are rarely teaching the woke ideology in an overt way. William Clark's high school class is the exception, not the rule. Where it generally begins is a discussion of fairness and justice.

Here's an example from an actual class that I've witnessed:

Teacher: "Do you believe the last line of the Pledge of Allegiance that says, 'liberty and justice for all'?"
Class: "Yes!"
Teacher: "Well, do you think it's fair that some people have more than other people do?"
Class: "No!"
Teacher: "Exactly. And that's what we mean by equity—making sure that everyone has the same, because that's what's fair!"

In this nugget of classroom time that took less than five minutes, the teacher has introduced the idea of equity versus equality. As we covered earlier, this is the difference between equality of opportunities and equality of outcomes.

From here, the teacher could go in several directions:

- They could teach that different racial groups have different outcomes and use systemic racism as the obvious explanation for it. They will use cherry-picked data as confirmation, without exposing students to the full nuance of the discussion.
- They could also talk about privilege as being a reason that different groups start in different places, ignoring that in a free society, you will always have some individuals in more advantageous positions than others based on individual merit and work ethic.
- And, when the students agree that they would prefer a system where everyone has the same thing, the teacher

> could use that as a chance to discuss anti-racism as a solution to the obvious inherent problems.

As you're reviewing homework, you must be on the lookout for the small things, not the big gestures. Don't get me wrong, if your little angel brings home a worksheet that says, "Be less white," shout that from the rooftops! But most of the time, it will be more subtle. As you practice and learn more about what to look for, you'll be able to pick out the patterns in no time.

Document everything you find and use it to fight back.

*Spy on the teacher's social media*. In June 2021, a mom from Carmel, NY, named Tatiana Ibrahim went viral for getting up at a school board meeting airing her concerns about the political leanings of the teachers in the schools and how those influences were making their way into the classroom. And part of the reason she knew what was happening was because the teachers were posting what they were doing on their public social media accounts.

If you want to know what the people teaching your kids believe, you need to see what they're posting on their Twitter, Instagram, TikTok, and so on. Screenshot everything that is the least bit suspicious, because you may need it later.

It is important to be judicious when engaging in espionage like this. First, teachers are allowed to express beliefs in their private lives. Teachers are allowed to support Black Lives Matter personally. They are allowed to do any anti-racism activities they want personally. If they hold these beliefs personally, that does not mean they are absolutely, 100 percent, definitely bringing it into the classroom.

But sometimes teachers get so cocky that they show you exactly what they are teaching your children on the internet for the sake of gaining virtue points. They post lessons or materials they are giving out to students with a BLM fist on it. And that's when you can really nail them to the wall. A teacher is allowed to hold individual beliefs—they are not allowed to bring those individual beliefs into the classroom.

*Review your state's teacher licensure requirements.* In February 2021, the Joint Committee on Administrative Rules of the Illinois General Assembly ratified a rule requiring "Culturally Responsive Teaching and Leading" standards. These are new rules that address how teachers should assess their own biases and how those biases might make them act racist, sexist, homophobic, and so forth. You get the idea.

This is an example of a state formalizing the woke ideology into practice. Don't be surprised if we don't start seeing more of this, and make sure you do a quick search (use DuckDuckGo, not Google) to look at the requirements in your state. You have to make sure you know what you're up against and what the teachers have really been up to when you haven't been looking. That information can be additional evidence for what is going on in the schools. You can also use it to make sure your lawmakers are aware of what is going on so they can push back.

*Form a group for concerned parents.* As you're reviewing homework and spying on social media, you'll probably find examples that make you feel uncomfortable with the state of education in your schools. At that point, you may want to call for reinforcements.

I know it can be frightening to start by going public, but per actively unwoke rule #9, it can really help to have social support. So, start with something more private—a small group of parents who can talk to each other, even if it's just you and one other parent.

Here's how you find out who might be on your team: call up some of your fellow parents and show them some of the examples you're finding of questionable homework or social media posts and simply ask them what they think of it.

When you do this, how you approach it is very important. Don't talk about politics. Don't talk about Critical Race Theory. Don't use any buzzwords. Just look at the assignment and walk them through what might be wrong about it.

- Does it call all cops bastards?
- Does it say the police came from slave catchers and therefore we should defund modern-day police forces?
- Does it talk about destroying capitalism?
- Does it make them write an essay about equity versus equality?
- Does it advocate for Black Lives Matter or the 1619 Project?

Yes, all of these are real examples.

Maybe the parent on the other end of the phone says they find it questionable and maybe they don't. But if they do, that's a potential ally.

Once you've got your group, figure out which ways work best to communicate and coordinate your efforts. And if everyone keeps bringing friends into the group, soon you will have an army.

*Speak out at school board meetings.* Never think a local school board meeting can't have a major impact. In July 2021, an article appeared on Politico titled "Could a School-Board Fight

Over Critical Race Theory Help Turn Virginia Red?" Parents in Loudoun County, Virginia, had been waging an epic struggle against their own school board's adoption of CRT. (The board had even spent $34,000 on fifty-five hours' worth of Critical Race Theory coaching according to public documents.) The fight had started to make national news, especially after an angry mob of parents entirely shut down one of the meetings in June. Every single time a school board fight makes the news, you inspire more parents and concerned citizens to speak out.

When you go public, school boards are your first stop for having a direct line into the schools. Remember, you are entitled to be heard. Your taxes pay for everything in that school. The very worst thing that happens is you speak your mind and get a thing or two off your chest. The very best thing that happens is you inspire change. You may have to go back more than once for that to be achieved, but once you do, it will get easier the second time around.

And when you go to the meetings, film *everything*. Yes, I know you might not be comfortable being on camera, but it is always better to have footage and to make the choice not to use it than it is to not have footage and wish you did. Videos of parents fighting back at school board meetings have earned millions of viral views and received coverage on major news networks. They are an extremely effective tool.

Better yet, *run* for a school board position and become a part of the decision-making process. In fact, you can run for school board even if you don't have kids! Your taxes pay for the school, regardless of whether you utilize it or not. Justice Graves is a young man from Templeton, MA, who joined my Locals online community determined to make a difference and fight back against Critical Race Theory in his hometown.

He didn't have kids, but that didn't mean he didn't care about the direction of the country. He ran for, and successfully won, a spot on the school committee, gaining over 60 percent of the vote on an anti-CRT platform. If he can do it, what's stopping you?

## Lobby Your State Representatives

Because public schools are funded by our taxes, we can begin to pull out the big guns and demand legislation. There are a few different types of bills that can provide added protections against the woke in schools, which we'll cover over the next few sections:

- Banning the teaching of divisive concepts (Critical Race Theory) in state agencies, state contractors, and government-funded schools.
- Educational transparency bills to require teachers to post online the materials they are using in classes.
- Bills supporting school choice by funding students directly rather than schools to provide parents with more options for educating their child.
- Putting #CamerasInClassrooms to give parents a way to monitor what teachers are really teaching.

Let's start with the easiest: laws banning divisive concepts.

Make sure you know the laws in your state regarding Critical Race Theory and other divisive concepts in schools. And if your state doesn't have a law yet, now is the perfect time to contact your state representatives and lobby for the idea. We're lucky that now we have several templates to choose from—just look at the examples from any of the states who have implemented legislation to this effect, including Idaho, Tennessee, Oklahoma, Iowa, and New Hampshire as of this writing. (But check the status of any legal challenges that may surround these laws, because it may have shifted in the meantime.)

Even better yet, use the parents group you may have created already to lobby collectively. This is a numbers game, and your job when you're lobbying for a bill is to show that you have the numbers on your side. Coordinate to send as many emails as possible, make as many phone calls as possible, and throw a rally outside of your state house. When I was supporting the anti-CRT bill in New Hampshire when it was still in committee, I got over two thousand emails sent supporting the bill simply by pleading with as many people as I possibly could to send a message supporting it. One lawmaker told me they literally received an email every single minute supporting the bill to their committee inbox. The numbers matter—these are the things lawmakers pay attention to.

Remember that you don't need a social media presence to do this. Maybe you get five friends to send an email, then they get five friends each, and then those friends get five friends. Before you know it, you're in the thousands. Because every one of these bills is deeply controversial, you will face a lot of opposition. They will lie about what the bill says. They will try to smear the lawmakers who are sponsoring it. Pay it no mind and keep your eye on the prize. Follow actively unwoke rules #4 and #5—don't be afraid to get in their face and tell them the truth.

## Academic Transparency

The next logical place for legislation that would get schools back in order is the educational transparency department. Though less popular than anti-CRT/divisive concepts bills, these bills might actually be more effective in continuing to expose corruption in the public schools than the ones banning Critical Race Theory.

For instance, in May 2021, HB 755 was introduced in North Carolina that created new reporting requirements for all K-12 public schools to provide information by the end of the school year regarding the lesson plans utilized that year, including an outline of the teacher's instructions, a list of course materials, and an outline of all activities in the classroom, including guest presenters.

The benefit of the COVID lockdowns was that parents finally had direct access to see precisely what their students were learning. With schools moving back to in-person instruction and teachers more on guard than ever due to the anti-CRT laws, these laws will push for the preservation of transparency.

## Put #CamerasInClassrooms

One night in May 2021, I was lying in bed around midnight, and I tweeted out a simple question: If any dog owner could log onto a phone app and check in on their pet in doggy day care, then why wouldn't it be possible to put a camera in every American classroom so that parents can watch what the teachers are teaching their children?

I fell asleep shortly after sending the tweet, not thinking much of it. The next morning, I woke up to discover it was going viral with over two million views. My feed was FILLED with leftists angry at the mere late-night suggestion that cameras should record what teachers are teaching.

And that's when I knew there was something to this idea. I've been canceled by the left more than once, and I had never seen them get so fired up about an idea. They were viscerally angry, getting bent more and more out of shape every moment. If something as simple as a tweet infuriates the left to that extent, that means you're on-target.

Thus #CamerasInClassrooms was born, because if the left is genuinely infuriated by an idea, it is absolutely worth considering. It's not a brand new idea—parents of special needs children have pushed for it before. But the context has changed, and the need for it is greater than ever.

Think about it for a moment. We have an insurmountable problem when it comes to the public education system in this county. It will take generations to fix unless we accelerate dramatically. One way to accelerate things is to wake more parents up to what is going on and what the schools are actually teaching their children.

And the best way to do that (even better than the educational transparency bill we just discussed) is to give parents a direct look into the classroom in real time. We can put a camera on every public school teacher in America so that they can be accountable to producing better results.

Give more parents access, and you will wake more parents up. As a bonus, teachers were working entirely online from the start of the pandemic and well into the following year—they were already doing for a full year plus exactly what

#CamerasInClassrooms would do, so they can't complain about privacy concerns.

When the left mobbed me for daring to suggest this idea, it presented a wonderful opportunity to pressure test the idea and figure out the flaws so I could answer them. As the day went on, it became clear that not a single argument was brought up that should legitimately dissuade from the idea of #CamerasInClassrooms.

*Worried about having cameras on your children?* Your children are already filmed all the time. Many day cares have cameras that parents can check on. They're filmed on school buses. They're filmed in school hallways. They're filmed if they're playing in basketball games, in the school play, or a band recital. They're filming each other from the moment you buy them a cell phone. Why is a camera on their teacher in the classroom a step too far?

*But what about their privacy? Students deserve privacy!* I hate to be a Debbie Downer, but public schools are paid for by the taxpayer—they are not a private space. *Plock v. Board of Education of Freeport School District No. 145* says, "A classroom in a public school is not the private property of any teacher.... There is nothing private about communications which take place in such a setting."

And again, your kids are already being filmed there anyway. But here's some reassurance—the goal of putting #CamerasInClassrooms is not to watch students. It's to watch teachers. The camera could be pointed at the front of the classroom, and there must be technology to only record audio for the teacher, not for the students. Sure, students may appear on camera every now and again, but if the recordings are only shared with parents of children in the class, not the general public, isn't that a sacrifice we should be willing to make given the broader context?

*What about the teacher's right to free speech?* Teachers have neither the right to privacy nor to free speech when they are acting in their capacity as public school teachers in government schools. This is something the Supreme Court has already ruled on—teachers do not have First Amendment protections when they are acting as teachers because they are employees of the state. They do have protections when they are acting as private citizens.

*You just want a surveillance state!* The greatest trick the teachers' union ever played was convincing us that public school teachers are not government employees. In this scenario, the state is literally the thing being surveilled. Public school teachers are employees of the state, and they must be held accountable for what they are teaching. We have a right to film state employees—cops wear body cams. Besides, teachers have already been teaching online for a full year! How is this any different than continuing to broadcast their classes live on the internet?

*Why are you punishing all teachers?* I've heard from many teachers who would welcome #CamerasInClassrooms. It would actually help them if they had their lessons recorded so that they could share them with students after the fact or even send them home to students who are sick so they don't really need to miss school. Good teachers should *want* to give parents more access to the classroom. If teachers don't want parents to see what they are teaching, parents should probably be asking what they are afraid of!

*No, this will just make more helicopter parents.* Remember that story about teachers creating fake curricula to send home to parents earlier in this chapter? Remember all the examples of teachers blatantly saying they would flout the law and teach Critical Race Theory regardless? You'll have to pardon me but what the hell? Parents are entrusting their children to teachers. They are paying the taxes that pay for the schools and everything in them. And they have every right to know exactly what is being taught and should have the ability to ask whatever questions they like of people who spend more time with their kids than anyone else.

There is no solution I can think of that would accelerate the demise of Critical Race Theory and the woke indoctrination system that is the public schools faster than #CamerasInClassrooms. The minute that parents can see exactly what their kids are learning is the minute the game changes in our favor. Right now, they can lie to themselves and think, "It's not happening in my town." Take away their ability to do that, and we wake a lot of people up.

Finally, #CamerasInClassrooms might have an auxiliary outcome as well. The Hawthorne effect is the idea that if we know we're being watched, that might be enough to change our behavior. Well, what if putting #CamerasInClassrooms is enough to change teacher behavior? What if they know they will be held accountable for teaching what to think, not how to think? What would happen the first time a teacher got fired for teaching something they weren't supposed to? It would send a message to all other teachers to cut it out. They wouldn't need to like it, they'd just need to do it. The ones who don't want to can quit and take their activism elsewhere.

This is an idea you can propose. Propose it to other parents at your school. Propose it with the school board. Propose it to the state legislature. Plant the seeds and advocate for the idea locally. This could be the game changer we need, but it only works when people get involved and demand it. Make sure you get in the game.

## Defund the Public Schools

When I was young and idealistic, I thought we should invest as much money in the public schools as possible, giving every teacher everything they needed to teach the next generation of leaders. Any suggestion of vouchers, educational freedom accounts, or school choice was completely antithetical to my world view, and I dismissed them out of hand without even considering how revolutionary they could be. And homeschooling? Ugh! I thought that was just for weird overly religious families with at least six children.

Oh, what a difference a decade and a massive red pill can make.

The government has proven they are completely incapable of properly educating children. Today's graduates are barely able to read and write at appropriate levels, let alone develop the skills they truly need to be productive members of society. Why are we continuing to pay into a system that is a failure based on every possible measure?

Defunding the schools would be a revolutionary act, but it may be the only act that is truly enough to get things back on track. That type of change can be scary, but sometimes scary change is what is necessary. Maybe start smaller, by promoting funding that follows the student instead of going directly to the system and allow the free market to do its job.

I'm not an extremist by any stretch. But I can look at the reality of the situation we're in and know that small changes aren't going to do the trick. Until we get there, we must keep throwing sand in the gears in any way we can. This happened as a battle of inches on the side of the woke we can fight it in the same way.

Ultimately, the educational system of our unwoke society looks a lot different than the one that got us in this mess in the first place, and everyone should be ready for that.

# Corporate Takeover

On February 19, 2021, I received an email from a whistleblower inside Coca-Cola explaining that he had come into work to discover an email notifying them of a new diversity training curriculum called "Better Together" and directing them to complete a series of online trainings by April 9.

A part of the curriculum was a course hosted on LinkedIn Learning called "Confronting Racism: Understanding What It Means to be White, Challenging What it Means to be Racist" featuring the work of the infamous Robin DiAngelo.

The whistleblower sent me a series of slides from the LinkedIn Learning platform with Coke's icon in the upper right-hand corner, indicating they were logged in under an official corporate account. The slides said that in the US and other Western nations, white people are socialized to feel that they are inherently superior because they are white, that research shows children start to believe it's better to be white at three years old, and that to be white is to be oppressive, arrogant, certain, defensive, ignorant, to not be humble, to not listen, and to exist with "white solidarity."

But the last slide was the clincher, having just five simple words: *Try to be less white.*

Because this training was available on LinkedIn Learning, I double-checked the content to make sure it was real. Sure enough, it was. One of the largest companies in the world was utilizing a training that explicitly told employees to be less white.

Without hesitating another moment, I blasted out the following tweet: "BREAKING: Coca-Cola is forcing employees to complete online training telling them to 'try to be less white,'" and included the whistleblower's images that were sent to me.

I've been on Twitter since 2007, and I have never seen a single tweet take off like this one did. It immediately started going viral, attracting the attention and retweets from every major conservative influencer, members of Congress, and major news outlets. Thousands of memes were generated making fun of "Woka-Cola" (the ones with the iconic polar bears learning they needed to be less white were particularly hilarious). Songs were written about it, including a line in Tom MacDonald's epic track "Snowflakes." Coca-Cola changed their outgoing voice message at their corporate headquarters to address the training, calling it "erroneous reporting." I even discovered that it was being discussed by human resource professionals who were not involved in politics at all and couldn't believe these slides were showing up in a workplace presentation. Since, generally speaking, HR pros are among the wokest of the woke in any organization, you know you've gone too far when they're questioning you!

It became a moment that truly influenced culture and brought awareness to the problem in a new way as the most overt example of what the woke ideology stands for. In total, that single tweet got 27.5 million views. Don't let anyone convince you that one simple act (like sending a tweet) can't make a difference. The "Be Less White" training proves that is simply untrue.

When opportunities like this present themselves, we have to be focused and milk them for everything they are worth. The truth is we just don't get many chances like this, and it's important to take advantage of every single one of them, even when doing so might be scary. I happened to suddenly have a very large microphone shoved in front of me, and I was going to use it to the best of my ability to enact change.

Coca-Cola issued two statements on the matter. In the first statement, they confirmed the existence of the training but said it was part of their larger "Better Together" program. A few hours later, they issued a second statement denying the training was ever a part of their program. Whether it was or wasn't didn't matter as much, so far as I was concerned. (Although I did hear from my whistleblowers that Coke immediately scrubbed the training from their internal website to avoid further blowback.) My target was much bigger: the LinkedIn Learning platform that hosted the training.

This is a critical example of when we need to keep our eye on the target and always be mindful of our goal—yes, making memes about Coke is fun, entertaining, and can influence perception, but that doesn't mean we give up on chances to have more concrete wins.

LinkedIn Learning is one of the largest corporate learning platforms in the world, meaning that this training was not only accessible to employees at Coke but at large and small organizations all over the world. A simple review of LinkedIn showed employees from Microsoft, the Philadelphia Eagles, Singapore Airlines, the Democratic National Committee, Adidas, Santander Bank, Walmart, LEGO, Carhartt, Nokia, the Seattle Police Department, Blue Cross Blue Shield, Tiffany & Co., Verizon, Dropbox, and more were all taking this training. It is, of course, unclear whether their companies were mandating they complete the training or if they stumbled across it on their own while utilizing the platform for other professional development. Regardless, the existence of the course on the platform was a far greater problem than any single company utilizing it.

I was featured on Glenn Beck's radio show the following day and used my time with him to try to redirect the conversation to where our attention should have been from the start: this course was hosted by one of the largest corporate training platforms in the world. I'm not sure if a producer on Tucker Carlson's show heard my chat with Glenn or if they got to that conclusion by themselves, but that evening Tucker hosted a segment about the training where he focused more on LinkedIn than he did on Coke. Less than three hours after this segment aired, the training was taken down from LinkedIn Learning. This was one of the first high-profile wins we earned in the fight against Critical Race Theory.

## Not All Diversity Training Is Created Equal

As an organizational psychologist, corporate training is something I'm intimately familiar with. I started my own business in this world in 2012 as a part-time side hustle while I was working on my PhD and eventually went full-time with it in 2015. My training specialty is how to communicate with people who have different work styles to enhance team cohesion, productivity, and engagement; how managers can create awesome work environments for their employees; and even training on how to utilize mindfulness strategies at work to reduce personal stress and enhance well-being. My first book, called *Zen Your Work*, deals with the mindfulness piece.

I'm also intimately familiar with the workplace professional development community, having been featured as a keynote speaker at multiple events for the largest HR organization in the world, the Society for Human Resource Management (SHRM). I first noticed diversity trainings starting to gain steam around 2017 when more and more presentations on the topic were making their way into the HR conferences I was attending.

At first, I didn't think too much of it. As a general rule, I don't have a problem with diversity training in the workplace. There's nothing wrong with people learning about different life experiences and perspectives so they can be more mindful of how they are communicating with people. That's the tactic that many (though not all) diversity trainings used to take—simply explore different life experiences without attempting to vilify the dominant group for those experiences. To this day, I have absolutely no problem with organizations choosing to engage with these types of diversity trainings. There's not a whole lot of evidence that they lead to tangible improvements, but there's not a whole lot of evidence that they hurt team cohesion either. As long as no damage is being done to individuals and teams, no harm, no foul.

But then I started to hear about microaggressions. As a reminder, a microaggression can best be defined as a time when any white person says anything that might offend any non-white person in the oppression hierarchy that we discussed earlier in the book. Any microaggression is thought to reveal unconscious bias that you have against the person; you are directing the microaggression based on their immutable characteristics.

- Forget to CC a person of color on an email about something that might peripherally involve them? Microaggression.
- Ask someone with an accent where they are from? Microaggression.
- Leaving a person of color out of a meeting or not rescheduling it around their calendar if they have a conflict? Microaggression.
- Pointing out you have non-white friends when an ally demands you shut up and listen to black people? Microaggression.
- Pointing out that COVID came from China? Microaggression.
- Denying white privilege is a real thing? BIG microaggression.

The idea was invented by a professor at Columbia University named Derald Wing Sue who, coincidentally, is the only person I've been able to find who has written papers in support of the idea of microaggressions being a real thing. All of the other research I've seen on the subject told me that there was no way to know if something that was considered a microaggression for one person would impact another person in the same way. If there's no provable consistency in how the phenomenon shows up, it's not something we should be treating as a serious concept.

But Derald Wing Sue does, and he makes a ton of money consulting with organizations and institutions who pay him to help them rid their employees' deep, unconscious bias. Sue would likely point to microaggressions like a white person asking to touch the hair of a black person, assuming that someone is an immigrant purely because of their skin color, or a white person calling the cops on a black child for having an unpermitted lemonade stand on the side of the road. These things do happen and, let's be honest, lack a certain sensitivity to the issues at play.

However, those examples aside, the vast majority of the times that I encountered the idea of microaggressions in the workplace were for the most innocuous actions that, prior to the current craze, would simply have been classified as miscommunications between colleagues that could be easily solved with a simple conversation. All of a sudden, accusations of racism over minor infractions proliferated in the work environment.

**Pop quiz**: If a colleague reports you to HR for being a racist because you forgot to include them on an email chain discussing the office holiday party, are you likely to have a productive working relationship with that person?

Yeah, probably not.

Anytime I saw these ideas show up on a team, I knew I was in for a challenging experience because call-out culture (one where you are constantly identifying different microaggressions to "call out" your co-workers) is extremely toxic to the psychological safety of any working group. According to a two-year study conducted at Google (before the woke took over), psychological safety is the number one driver of team success because it means that team members feel comfortable supporting each other and even failing in front of each other. That allows them to effectively work through the most challenging experiences more productively. When psychological safety is broken on a team, it can create all sorts of interpersonal problems that can have a real effect on their bottom-line work.

After microaggressions, I started to hear about the idea of organizations having a "white supremacy culture." A group called dRworks ("dR" stands for "dismantling racism") produced a PDF called "white supremacy culture" in the late 2000s, but it took about ten years for it to make its way into a critical mass of organizations.

Here are some characteristics of a "white supremacy culture" according to this group:

- Perfectionism: Pointing out what's wrong with someone's work instead of gushing about what's right.
- Sense of urgency: Moving fast and not including everyone's opinions into the decision-making process.
- Defensiveness: Considering new ideas with skepticism, making it more difficult for new ideas to be raised.
- Quantity over quality: Placing a priority on quantifiable measurements over how people feel about the decisions.
- Worship of the written word: Memorializing things in a memo or other written documentation.

- Only one right way: The belief that your way is the correct way to do something.
- Individualism: The desire to get credit for your work.
- Objectivity: Believing that a person can be objective or neutral.
- Right to comfort: Using logic over emotions to make decisions.

Every single one of those bullet points, along with dozens more I left out for the sake of brevity, are deemed characteristics of white supremacy. Any average Joe off the street can probably quickly identify that none of those points have anything to do with the race of a person—anyone of any race is perfectly capable of writing a memo!

When I saw this paper, I immediately noticed something else: almost every single characteristic noted aligned with a Dominant work style on the DISC model that we explored earlier. (By pure coincidence, I'm sure, but it also happens to be the work style I most closely associate with Donald Trump.) Every single work style has both strengths and weaknesses, and we need people with the Dominant style on teams because they provide direction for the rest of us. Without them, we'd never get anywhere! But this document took some of their most challenging traits and labeled them as tools of white supremacy.

If you're wondering why they might choose one work style to target for their accusation of racism, let's remember what their true goal is: obtaining power. People with the Dominant work style are much more likely to rise to the top of organizations because of their natural inclination to want to be in leadership positions. They are also much more likely than other styles to call the woke out on their bullshit. So, of course, they must be targeted by the woke—they are using it to gain ways to influence their decision-making processes.

These two topics—microaggressions and diversity, equity and inclusion training—started gaining more and more traction in the HR and professional development space. In late 2019, it looked like 2020's major theme was shaping up to be the year of diversity training.

## And Then George Floyd Died

The year 2020 certainly did a number on the workplace. When the pandemic started, I had already prebooked enough business for the year to fund my practice and was on track to have record-breaking profit. All of that was wiped out in a matter of weeks as companies moved their operations online, and no one was doing in-person workshops or presentations any longer. I mitigated it for a while by focusing on online coaching and training programs.

The real game changer for my industry was the death of George Floyd. In an instant, the only thing organizations were hiring for was anti-racist training, otherwise known as the bad kind of diversity training that is almost always grounded in Critical Race Theory and drives teams apart rather than brings them together. This type of training became a mandatory virtue signal that organizations made to their woke employees and consumers as a way of saying, "Don't hurt us." And why wouldn't they—every night we were greeted on the evening news with stories of looting and rioting across the country that were destroying businesses. Don't want to have a social media mob come after your business? You better do that anti-racist training.

Here are some examples of ways that anti-racist training shows up in the workplace:

- Sandia National Laboratories sent its white male executives to a reeducation retreat called "White Men's Caucus on Eliminating Racism, Sexism, and Homophobia in Organizations." Among other things, they were forced to write apology notes for being both white and male, even if their behaviors had not been racist or sexist.
- Employees at Cigna were taught that people were "privileged" if they are able-bodied, aged twenty-five to fifty-five, Christian, cis-gendered, heterosexual, upper class, male, and (of course) white. They were also told to eliminate phrases like "brown bag lunch," "grandfathered," and "no can do" from their vocabulary at work because they weren't inclusive enough.
- Disney instituted a diversity training program called "Reimagine Tomorrow" in which they told employees that the United States has a "long history of systemic racism and transphobia" and that white employees should "work through feelings of guilt, shame, and defensiveness to understand what is beneath them and what needs to be healed." They also instructed them not to expect their black colleagues to do the emotional labor to educate them.

If you work in corporate America today, chances are very high that your company has already instituted training based on these ideas, or they will be in the very near future. The severity of them will range from relatively harmless to overtly toxic.

## Be Actively Unwoke at Work

Particularly when it comes to your livelihood, it's important to be cautious and to go in with eyes wide open if you are pushing back. I'm all for speaking out. This entire book is about speaking out and standing up for what you believe in! However, in the workplace you have to play it a bit more cautiously because you don't want to put yourself in a situation of being on the receiving end of a pink slip.

The reality is that people have lost their jobs simply for asking if these trainings are a good idea—it is a very real possibility. Sometimes, the very best thing to do will be to grin and bear it, knowing the organization is just doing the training to check it off the list, and it won't likely have a long-term impact. But if you find your workplace getting more and more woke, there are ways you caught fight back without putting a target directly on your back. Here are some ideas.

*Realize you're not alone.* Let's go back to rule #9 again: social support can sometimes make all the difference in the world, especially in a situation when you might not be able to up and leave your job. It may be worthwhile to suss out who your allies are in the office.

When you're making small talk, you could mention whatever the current popular news stories are on the subject at the time you're reading this. For example, when Coke's "Be Less White" training came out, I might have said, "Did you hear about the 'Be Less White' training?" and utilized their answers to gauge a reaction of if they are a friend or foe. Always remember that there are more of us than there are of them, and when we stick together, we win.

*Know where your boss stands.* Even if your organization is implementing woke trainings and strategies, don't assume your boss is on board with all of it. Your boss can make all the difference and can be utilized as a buffer for the really bad stuff.

Use the same technique as the previous point to try to get a feel for where your boss stands. If you get the sense that they are on your side, you may consider expressing your discomfort with the direction of things in a one-on-one meeting. Don't do this with any sort of hostility or malice—keep it professional by stating you're worried the trainings will make collaboration worse instead of better, and offer alternative ideas. Remember that if your boss is unwoke, it might be a great relief for them to know there are others who feel the same way and could give them the courage they need to speak up to their manager.

Having an unwoke boss won't change everything your organization is doing, so you must manage your expectations. You'll likely still have to go to the diversity trainings, pay close attention not to say anything gendered, and go along with the woke office parties that are inevitable killers of all fun and joy. However, at least you can be sure that your day-to-day environment won't be hijacked, and sometimes that can make the rest of it a little more bearable.

*Ask purposefully dumb questions.* On June 16, 2020, James Lindsay posted a thread on Twitter targeted towards people who would soon have to endure anti-racist training at work. (View the full thread at bit.ly/antiracistquestions.) He suggests using "calibrated" questions, which is a much more diplomatic way of saying he suggests that you play dumb to both annoy the facilitator and simultaneously make the point to everyone listening that these ideas do not make sense. Act like a slow learner, as if you're just trying to figure out the ideas and aren't understanding. They include:

- "So, when you say 'racist' and 'anti-racist,' you don't mean, like, the normal definition?"
- "So, if I become an 'anti-racist,' am I still a racist? How does this program make me not racist?"
- "Wait, so if colorblindness means not seeing race, and that makes me racist, does seeing race make me racist? Is race supposed to matter or not matter?"
- "Doesn't making us focus on race more make the issue more sensitive, and doesn't a reporting system make it harder to work with people we don't trust?"

James notes that the more questions you ask, the more you are going to piss off the facilitator, so it's best to be measured in your approach. Sometimes pushing just a little bit to make your point is enough. Remember, your goal is not to convert the facilitator. That is a lost cause! Your goal is to plant seeds among the other people listening.

*Document EVERYTHING.* When your workplace sends out an email with their latest virtue signal, don't just glaze over it or automatically delete it. Give it a read. Make sure you know what they are saying. And then forward yourself a copy to your personal email (it's best if it's on a site like ProtonMail) for safe keeping. Every time your workplace does a crazy training, make sure you get a copy of the slide deck or (better yet) record it if you can.

Documentation will make sure you have a list of specific grievances that you can use to your advantage later (if you need to sue them for discrimination, let's say), but it will also allow you act as a whistleblower to expose what's going on. You can get in touch with people like me, Christopher Rufo, James Lindsay, or even Project Veritas and, depending on the severity of the materials, we may be able to help bring coverage to your situation to provide a little incentive for your company to do the right thing. You don't need to take the risk yourself—there are people who will help you. As we saw with the Coke "Be Less White" training example, a single act of defiance can have a great impact. To this day, the Coke whistleblower's identity has not been revealed. Look at what their efforts exposed.

*Infiltrate the diversity committee.* If you can't beat 'em, join 'em! One way to make a difference in your workplace is to get in the game and request to be on your organization's diversity committee. These are usually the people who are in charge of selecting the diversity trainings and activities. As we've discussed, there are diversity trainers out there who do an OK job and who won't bring the woke mindset or Critical Race Theory into your organization. If you need to do the training anyway, you may as well try to steer them in a direction that won't be detrimental. One member of my Locals online community (who shall remain nameless because she's still holding her position, and we don't want them to know she's not woke) actually got herself put in charge of creating the diversity plan for a very large organization, directly impacting the lives of thousands employees in the process!

*You can always look for greener pastures.* One of the great benefits of the pandemic is that because so many companies had to adjust to working virtually, they are more open than ever to hiring employees all over the world. If your company gets so woke that you feel like you can't take it anymore, get proactive. Dust off that resume, get in touch with recruiters, and start hustling to find your dream gig elsewhere. And on your way out, make sure they know why you left, either in the exit interview or by writing it into your letter of resignation.

Also, keep in mind that unless you are under a specific contract (or just want your vacation days paid out), you are under no obligation to give your employer any notice before quitting. The longer you hang around after you turn in your letter of resignation, the more time you give them to screw with you. I suggest getting ready to leave on the day and walking out the door with the swagger of a king.

## If You're in a Leadership Role, Act Like It

We used to believe that once the woke left college, the reality of the working world would fix whatever woke indoctrination they endured. However, sadly, far too many companies have decided to bend the knee to the woke employees in their ranks and give in to almost any demand that is made. Of course, they are thanked for their efforts with continued unfettered demands that never seem to go away. Remember rule #7 about not bending the knee—grant them a concession and they want three more after it.

But some CEOs are fighting back, refusing to let the direction of the organizations they've poured their blood, sweat, and tears into be dictated by a woke mob. The best way to get the demands to stop is to simply say, "NO." If you're in a leadership position in your organization, this is your time to shine.

You wouldn't be the first leader to declare your organization a politics-free zone.

The first high profile example was Red Bull. In July 2020, three hundred employees at Red Bull attempted to pressure the company to speak publicly regarding social justice and systemic racism, asserting that their silence in regard to the Black Lives Matter movement was complicity. Typically, a move like this would result in the company caving and doing what the employees demanded. However, what the employees apparently didn't consider is that Red Bull is owned by billionaire CEO Dietrich Mateschitz, who has enough money to be cancel-proof by anyone, much less his own employees.

So, when executives in their North America branch, including their CEO Stefan Kozak and President and Chief Marketing Officer Amy Taylor, began to take the company down the path of virtue signaling to BLM, forcing diversity hires, and exacerbating racial tension in the organization, they were summarily fired. Florian Klaass, the head of global culture marketing (and the person responsible for a training slight about "ignorant Americans" that was leaked to the press) was also removed from his position. To put the final nail in the woke coffin, Red Bull got rid of its cultural marketing programs entirely and issued the following statement: "We reject racism in every form, we always have, and we always will." Flawless victory.

Next up came crypto company Coinbase. In September 2020, CEO Brian Armstrong released a memo on the company blog stating emphatically that the company would be focusing on its mission of creating an open financial system and using cryptocurrency to bring economic freedom to the world. As such, he wrote, the company would not be engaging with any issues unrelated to that mission, including broader societal issues and political causes. A few days after the memo, Armstrong followed up with an email to employees offering a generous severance package including four to six months of pay and insurance coverage for anyone who did not want to work for a company that would not engage in political causes. He welcomed them to exit the company with a safety net while they searched for their next great adventure.

This was a boss move, a first-of-its-kind gut punch against woke employees that were distracting from the core mission of the organization. It also proved the point that it pays to take a stand. When the dust settled, only 5 percent of employees took the severance offer—one out of twenty.

This is a critical point to understand for organizational leaders—it might seem as though all of your employees are woke when the mob comes for you, but there are typically very few true believers who will follow through on their threats. Most people who sign onto open letters that make demands of organizational leadership are doing so to go along with the crowd. If you force the crowd to move in a different direction by creating clear boundaries (e.g., no politics at work), they will go along with that too.

Sadly, the transition may not be so easy if your hiring practices brought a bunch of woke employees into the company in the first place, but that doesn't mean it's not worth making the move. It just means there will be a bit more cleaning up to do. This is the lesson learned by Basecamp, a project management company that made the misstep of allowing their employees to engage in political conversations on the company platform. In April 2021, CEO Jason Fried issued a statement declaring there would be "no more societal or political discussions on our company Basecamp account":

> "Today's social and political waters are especially choppy. Sensitivities are at 11, and every discussion remotely related to politics, advocacy, or society at large quickly spins away from pleasant. You shouldn't have to wonder if staying out of it means you're complicit, or wading into it means you're a target. These are difficult enough waters to navigate in life, but significantly more so at work. It's become too much. It's a major distraction. It saps our energy, and redirects our dialog towards dark places. It's not healthy, it hasn't served us well. And we're done with it on our company Basecamp account where the work happens. People can take the conversations with willing co-workers to Signal, Whatsapp, or even a personal Basecamp account, but it can't happen where the work happens anymore."

Just like Coinbase, Basecamp also offered its employees a generous severance package if they no longer felt they could come in and do their best work in the organization. However, they may not have anticipated that a much larger percent of employees would accept the offer—approximately twenty out of the company's fifty-seven employees took them up on it.

This may seem like a massive loss, but consider the following: in any organization, the distraction of one problematic employee will inhibit the impact of two rock stars. Basecamp may have lost roughly one-third of their staff in one fell swoop, but try looking at it like this: Basecamp got rid of all their problematic employees at once. They opened the door to bringing new talent on their team who would agree with the "no politics" rule up front and set up the company as a whole to refocus on its core mission.

Sometimes, you don't even have to go as far as offering them severance. James Lindsay notes that one strategy towards weeding out the woke is to meet their demands by making some of your own, and requiring responsibility and accountability. If a woke employee demands you hire more people of color, just say, "Great. It's your job to go find them (responsibility). If you don't do it in six months, you're fired (accountability)." Lindsay notes that 100 percent of the time he's seen this tactic implemented, the woke employee ends up quitting. The woke want neither responsibility nor accountability, even though they frequently demand it from others. All they want is to complain. Allow them to self-select themselves out by demanding both.

Here's the moral of the story: you don't have to stand by and watch wokism take over your workplace. It will distract from the mission, create interpersonal issues among the staff, reduce overall team cohesion and productivity. Every single business metric will go down when wokism is introduced. Regardless if your personal politics are left, right, or center, you have a fiduciary responsibility to your organization to put a stop to it.

## Companies Set Themselves Up for Failure When They Go Woke

Listen, I know this chapter isn't as sexy as some of the others. I'm not telling you to organize protests or write open letters denouncing your company leadership like the woke will typically do. That's because we have to play this smart, and I don't want to give you advice that could easily result in you losing your job. The struggle is real when it comes to consequences for speaking out, and you want to tread lightly. If we don't take care of our basic needs (like the security provided by a steady paycheck), it's much more difficult to focus on the bigger picture. You and your family must always come first, and if that means living to fight another day, so be it. No single person is under any obligation to take all of the burden on themselves. Look for opportunities to throw sand in their gears when you can (especially when it comes to documenting and releasing the woke trainings!), but never feel guilty if you can't do more to fight back in the workplace because you want to protect your job. Do what you can, and fight back in other ways outside of your company.

But if you've got financial security and don't mind taking the risk, then go for it! The reality is that you would be doing your company a favor by reminding them to focus on the mission rather than politics. This ideology doesn't make better teams—it only destroys them. It enters into organizations like a parasite that will take over and destroy any chance of business success. You can do a lot of people you work with a great favor by speaking up and demonstrating what bravery looks like, even if it means you take the bullet for a lot of them. You never know who you'll inspire by doing the right thing.

# State-Sanctioned Racism

Jennifer Friend was working as a clinical social worker in Fairfax County, Virginia. A fifteen-year veteran of the county's Community Services Board, she provided therapy and case management for county residents with severe mental illnesses and/or substance abuse disorders.

Then one day, her taxpayer-funded organization jumped on the equity bandwagon, launching the One Fairfax equity policy, designed to address the impact of systemic racism in the county. Included in this initiative was a diversity, equity, and inclusion website that included the following resources for employees to utilize:

- An article called "Save the Tears: White Woman's Guide," which noted that white women will utilize their tears in order to get the police to murder black people if white women ask them to and demanding said women consider the weight of that power.

- An anti-racism resources section featuring dozens of articles and resources, including an article titled "103 Things White People Can Do for Racial Justice" which encouraged employees to share information about defunding the police.
- An article titled "Answering White People's Most Commonly Asked Questions about the Black Lives Matter Movement" that included answers to questions like "Is defunding or abolishing the police really the answer?", which supported the idea of abolishing the police force with the following quote: "Abolition may feel like an extreme answer to you right now. That makes sense. You've been socialized to think that police 'protect and serve' and are a necessary presence for our common life together. But try on the idea that abolition doesn't mean anarchy, but intentionality." The article later said that "Many white people…are raised with the idea that calling the police is heroic. We must unlearn this."

Jennifer was particularly perturbed by the resources regarding police being framed in a negative way because, as a social worker, the police were a resource for the work that she and others in the organization were doing within the community. Think about that for a moment: a government organization was using its resources to encourage government employees to consume materials with an anti-police bent to them. This was all done in the name of advancing equity (equality of outcomes).

First, Jennifer raised concerns internally. In response, she was invited to a Zoom meeting with a human resources staff member to discuss her "communication around a very sensitive matter of race and equity." Sensing exactly how this conversation would go, she took the bull by the horns and sent an email to the entire Community Services Board stating her concerns. The organization responded to everyone, declaring that Jennifer's email contained multiple inaccuracies (it didn't) and asserting that the One Fairfax program would recognize the presence of institutional and structural racism.

Upon seeing the response, Jennifer publicly resigned. She was immediately cut off from further internal communication—but that didn't stop her from posting videos of what she found on YouTube and making sure she sent copies to the county chief of police, the County Board of Supervisors, the county executive, and Bolster the Blue, a police support network.

This communication earned Jennifer a rebuke from a county executive stating, "I am hopeful the posting of internal documents does not violate our use policy signed by all employees."

Jennifer responded with the ultimate badass, stand-your-ground, never-bend-the-knee answer: "I am likewise hopeful that Fairfax County Government posting racist, misogynistic and anti-police materials and encouraging government employees to view these materials is also not violating any rules."

Today, she works with Counterweight, an organization dedicated to helping individuals who find themselves in exactly the same position she did.

## It's About Destabilizing the System

I have an old textbook sitting on my desk called *What You Should Know About Communism and Why*. Published in the 1960s, it used to be used for school-age children (probably around middle-school age, possibly younger, because kids were smarter in those days) to teach the evils of what happens when you give the state control over the means of production and, as an extension, the people, taking students on a journey from Lenin to Stalin to China and Russia. The final chapter of the text is called "America's Shield of Freedom," which states the following:

> "One freedom that communism can never allow is freedom to disagree with communism itself. To Americans, the freedom to disagree, to think for oneself, is one of the most basic freedoms of all."

It proceeds with a lesson about the Bill of Rights, explaining that our country will never be a communist utopia because "...our rights and freedoms do not change with changing leaders. Our Constitution and laws guarantee our freedoms against interference from good leaders or bad ones."

Someone might want to explain that to Jen Psaki, White House Press Secretary under Joe Biden, who declared in July 2021 that the White House was working with Facebook to censor any posts the administration considered problematic or to Ibram X. Kendi who has long advocated for an anti-racist amendment to the Constitution that would establish and permanently fund a Department of Anti-Racism (with the appropriate acronym DOA). They may want to explain it to the educators who have taken it upon themselves to teach children in government schools what to think instead of how to think. They may want to explain it to the elected leaders (mostly Democrats but many Republicans too) who seem to believe that it's acceptable to revoke our constitutionally protected liberties in the case of a virus.

Today, the ideals discussed in a child's textbook fifty years ago are in very real danger. A quick review of something we discussed earlier in the book: The woke ideology and Critical Race Theory are not about race. They are about power. Everything the woke says and does is about gaining power and destabilizing our system, bit by bit. The goal is not creating a more fair and equitable society. It is revolution. We're in the middle of it right now.

The picture I'll paint for our government is just as bad as the one I painted for our schools: an entirely corrupted system. I'm not a revolutionary by any stretch of the imagination, but you don't have to be an anarchist to acknowledge that the checks and balances the founders put in place are very close to being subverted by the woke ideology that's been working its way into power for decades.

I've already mentioned Chris Rufo a few times in this book, but I'll gush about him again because he's done more work than just about anyone to bring public awareness to what is going on inside the government. Here are just a few of his investigations:

- The Treasury Department held a training session telling employees that "virtually all White people contribute to racism" and demanding staff accept their white privilege and fragility. The man who gave the training has billed the federal government more than $5 million for training over the past fifteen years.

- The National Credit Union Administration held a session for almost nine thousand employees arguing that America was founded on racism.
- The Department of Homeland Security hosted trainings on microaggressions that told white employees they had been socialized to be oppressors.
- The FBI has an Office of Diversity and Inclusion that hosts weekly intersectionality workshops.
- Lockheed Martin, one of the nation's largest defense contractors, sent their white male executives to a three day reeducation camp to deconstruct white male culture and atone for the sin of white male privilege. Raytheon, the second largest defense contractor, launched its own anti-racism program.

These are all examples from the federal government, but as we saw with Jennifer Friend's good work, it's at all levels down to your local town hall.

## Be Actively Unwoke and Fight the State

Many of the techniques that we've discussed in the previous two chapters can work for the state as well, so I won't rehash those here. Instead, I want to focus on things you can do specifically to fight back against the state-sanctioned woke indoctrination of its citizens.

*Stop voting for candidates who suck.* I don't know why this needs to be said, and yet here is where we will begin: if you do not want the country to go woke, then you have got to stop electing people who are allowing it to happen.

This is true if you are a Democrat. It's true if you are a Republican. It's true if you are an Independent, Libertarian, Green Party member, and so on. It doesn't matter what the letter next to your name is, you have got to stop voting for horrible candidates who are doing nothing but dragging us towards an authoritarian reality.

I have this conversation with those on the political right all the time:

Them: "We hate our politicians. They don't do anything we want them to do."
Me: "Then you might want to stop voting for them."
Them: "Well...they're still better than the Democrats."

In New Hampshire, my Republican in Name Only (RINO) governor Chris Sununu supported the Democrats when the Republicans in the state legislature introduced an anti-CRT bill. He tried to sabotage this bill every step of the way, getting his cronies, Attorney General John Formella and State Senator Jeb Bradley, to water down the bill for him to try to pander to the political left. What ultimately passed in New Hampshire was a shell of the bill that was introduced, and it was all Chris Sununu's fault.

Yet, he will almost certainly run for the United States Senate in 2022, and he will almost certainly do it with the full support of the Republican Party. He'll inevitably get the support of the GOP voters because the other guy is worse, even though the public schools in New Hampshire will still be indoctrinating their children because of him (whether it will be enough support to win him the seat remains to be seen).

And I'm sure I could have similar conversations on the left side of the aisle, who seem to have a penchant for electing authoritarians to office. Meanwhile, we're all sliding drastically down the slippery slope towards a dystopian reality, gaining more and more momentum all the time.

Let me be as blunt as possible: if you continue to vote for candidates who suck, they will always suck. Your vote has told them that it is OK for them to suck. The only way to force the major political parties to start offering up more candidates who do not suck is for them to know, emphatically, that they will lose if they do. Sometimes, you must suffer a short-term loss to gain a long-term victory. We're playing the long game here. This fight will not be won for generations, and it may not be won at all if we keep electing horrible candidates to office.

I'll come back to a statement I made at the beginning of the book: This is not about Democratic values or Republican values. This is about American values. If Americans aren't going to elect candidates who support American values, then what we get really is our own damn fault.

*Mind your language.* Language is one of the primary tools the woke use to maintain their power. It's a tool we can use to fight back as well. I find it's particularly effective in articulating the idea that our government overlords are encroaching on the rights of "we the people." Many people read *1984* at some point in their life and so likely have an idea of the dangers of a totalitarian state. However, many also seem to have trouble making the connection between the dystopian reality Orwell articulated in that novel and our progression to it today. We need to remind them.

Chris Rufo has advocated for calling Critical Race Theory in the federal government and in schools as "state-sanctioned racism." The term has since been used by Florida Governor Ron DeSantis and Senator Tom Cotton.

On May 11, 2020, school choice advocate Corey DeAngelis tweeted the following:

> Stop calling them "public" schools.
> They aren't open to the public.
> They aren't accountable to the public.
> They are run by government.
> They are regulated by government.
> They are funded by government.
> They are compelled by government.
> They are government schools.

These are just a few examples of how we can begin to use language to our advantage and turn their own ideas back around on them. Be mindful of using this language, and even come up with language of your own. If you find something that's effective at getting people's attention, make sure you share the ideas with others.

*Do not allow your speech to be compelled.* The government does not have constitutional protections—individuals do. And one of the things our First Amendment protects you from is the state compelling your individual speech. That means they can't force you to say anything.

If you work as a state employee, and they try to force your speech (say, by making you admit your inherent racism when you do not believe you are a racist as part of a government-funded, compelled training), they are violating your civil liberties, and you have the right to say no.

They may not like that you say no. They may even try to make you endure a struggle session. But if you believe in what you are standing up for, it is your obligation to stick to your guns and maintain your position.

Or, even better, follow Jennifer Friend's good example and use it as an opportunity to blow the whistle and educate the public about what our taxpayer dollars are funding. Blow the whistle, make it public. If it is funded by our tax dollars, the public has a right to know.

*File Right-to-Know and Freedom of Information Act requests.* If you work outside of the government, you still have a right to know what they are up to. Much of the reporting that has been done on the woke ideology in government organizations has come from these requests demanding documents regarding anti-racist and equity trainings occurring in taxpayer-funded organizations. You have every right to know what's going on, and there are tons of websites and resources to help you file these requests to make sure you are getting access to the information you need. And once you get them, of course, share them with the world!

*Speak up, protest, and rally.* In New Hampshire, everyone knows Lily Tang Williams. Lily is a Chinese immigrant and US citizen who grew up in China during Mao's Cultural Revolution and works tirelessly on her mission to make sure Americans are aware of the similarities between what she experienced growing up and what she sees happening in America today. She gives radio interviews, speaks to community groups and school-aged children, and is one of the loudest and most determined voices.

Many people are afraid of what will happen if they speak up. Lily speaks up because she is afraid of what will happen if she does not. She is an example of Asian Americans who are rallying as a part of the unwoke army, having direct experience with the damage this ideology can do. Lily started an organization called the New Hampshire Asian American Coalition and tirelessly advocated for the anti-CRT bill in New Hampshire in 2021, even organizing a successful rally at the State House in Concord to encourage the passage of the bill, and shined light on the dangers and reach of Critical Race Theory in the Granite State.

If you want elected officials to listen to you and your concerns, you have to show up. It's a numbers game, simple as that. This is a battle that will take place on a state level for the foreseeable future (at least until 2024, and we need to plan for it to be longer). Luckily, state and local officials tend to be more accessible.

You don't have to be the organizer of a rally to get involved. You just need to show up. I toured with the #WalkAway campaign during the 2020 election, speaking at rallies in blue cities all over the country to encourage people to leave the Democratic Party. Following each rally, many of us would hear from people who wish they would have come but suddenly had to mow their lawns at the exact time the rally was taking place. If things are important to you, then you will make it a priority to show up.

If you can't do that, at least reach out to your local and state representatives and make sure they know your concerns. Don't wait for someone to write you a template email—just find their official email address and write them a note in your own words, particularly if there is already legislation in progress that supports our work.

And if you can't do that, then you're not really in the fight, and I have to question how you made it this far into the book—these are the minimum things that need to happen and can be completed in just a few minutes of time. Remember all of the people who are out there fighting hard for you every day and get it done.

*Get involved or run for office.* One of the ways that the woke have gotten away with infiltrating the government is that they were simply the ones to show up. This is particularly true on the local level, where oftentimes you can get elected to a committee or to a school board just by showing up and rallying your friends to give you their vote. If you want to run for higher office on an anti-CRT platform, of course that's great too. However, do not underestimate the impact of these local offices.

Take the time to learn about what's going on in your local system of government. Join groups to help you get involved in politics and begin to connect with the players involved. Learn who your friends are and the people you need to watch out for. Inspect the social media of your local reps and know where they stand on these issues. Politics isn't for everyone, and lord knows sometimes it's a soul-sucking experience...but it can also be a lot of fun. And who knows, you might get yourself in a position to make a real difference along the way.

*Sue them.* The government plays by different rules than the private sector (and, yes, that includes the public "government" schools). One of the most important things we can work towards is the setting of a legal precedent and, if we're honest, it will probably take a trip to the Supreme Court to do it. (Let's hope that the conservative majority Trump installed survives!)

If you have a case against a government entity, it is your responsibility to explore your options with a lawyer. It's not just for you but for all of us. A few chapters ago, I told you the story of Gabrielle Clark suing her son William's school. Do you think Gabrielle—who is a single mother—woke up one day and said, "You know what? I'd like to start a lawsuit that will cost hundreds of thousands of dollars, put my family through the wringer, and take years of fighting before there's any hope of a win"? The answer is no, she did not. She did it because she knew a legal precedent was the most important battle in this fight, and her son has one of the most cut-and-dry cases of compelled speech that has been exposed to date.

Gabrielle showed up and sued because it was necessary, not because it was convenient.

## The Opposite of Authoritarian Is Libertarian

Other opposites might include liberal, populist, or free thinker.

Anarchist Michael Malice always says that conservatives are progressives driving the speed limit, and there is a lot of truth to that. After being a Democrat for twenty years, and then experiencing the Republican Party up close during the 2020 presidential campaign and the aftermath that followed, I am absolutely convinced that he is correct. We're already seeing Republicans (like Chris Sununu) basically tell us that the woke and Critical Race Theory aren't all that bad, pretending they don't understand that the state does not have free speech protections. We're seeing conservative influencers come out and say that maybe we shouldn't support laws to ban

CRT after all and let the free market of ideas take care of it. I absolutely believe that at this rate, the Republican Party will begin to openly support the woke ideology in the not-too-distant future.

The years that I've spent fighting the woke showed me very clearly that regardless of your official party registration status, the only group truly fighting back against the authoritarian power grab of the federal government is the Libertarians. And, for now, that's where I've landed in terms of my affiliation. I know that won't make the Republicans happy, but I truly believe that supporting the current structure of the GOP is not going to lead to us winning this fight. The woke are fighting for their revolution—the only way to truly combat that is with bold ideas and perhaps a more liberty-focused revolution of our own.

Yes, I know their last presidential candidate tweeted in support of Black Lives Matter, and she lost my vote because of it. No, I don't think the Libertarian Party (LP) is going to win any major elections anytime soon. Believe me, I understand there are many problems to solve within this party.

But I also know that joining the Mises Caucus within the LP has given me hope that they may actually be able to make their party act like Libertarians again and usher in a new Ron Paul revolution. And I also know that something must be done to pull back the power of the state from the establishment. If you don't know what the Mises Caucus is, check them out at takehumanaction.com. You might be surprised at what you find.

If a solid liberty candidate comes around in the Republican Party who has shown with their actions that they will fight back against the woke power grab, they could earn my vote.

And of course, if the LP nominates a sucky candidate who brings woke values to their platform, I won't touch them with a ten-foot pole. This is a time when we need to allow the best people to earn our support, not blindly vote for the people with the right letter next to their name.

# Turnabout Is Fair Play

Throughout this book, I've made the argument that we are in a cultural revolution. You don't stop a cultural revolution through laws banning divisive concepts. You don't stop it with lawsuits that go on for years and years before resolution. You stop a cultural revolution by changing the culture.

In order to change culture, you need bold messaging that pushes the envelope: messaging that jumps out in a sea of corporate advertising that we are inundated with every single day and messaging that cuts through the noise of the millions of hours of independent content that gets uploaded to the internet every day.

And sometimes the boldest messaging is (let's face it) a little bit naughty. It pushes the envelope. It exposes the dark underbelly of what this ideology really stands for.

So far in this book, we've focused on some pretty actionable strategies that play within the acceptable guidelines of the different institutions they were focused on. We've eaten our vegetables, now let's have some dessert. As long as we're following our actively unwoke rule #1 and staying within our values, then it's OK to follow our #2 rule: make the fight fun. Giving the woke a taste of their own medicine is just what the doctor ordered.

You can't fight dishonesty with politeness. The woke are dishonest. Maybe we need to stop being so polite.

Here are some fun ideas to get you started, but be creative. Experiment with your own ideas. Throw things at the wall and see what sticks. Learn from what works and what doesn't. And enjoy every single second of it.

## Call It What It Is

Critical Race Theory is a racist ideology. It is not just racist against white people; it is racist against everyone.

Critical Race Theory teaches that we must judge people and make assumptions about them based on the color of their skin. That's racist.

Critical Race Theory says that black people are incapable of going to the DMV and getting an ID, probably don't know how to use the internet, and are unwilling to work hard or be on time. That's racist.

When this nonsense theory is taught in schools, it teaches young black and brown children that they cannot be successful in life unless a white liberal goes out of their way to help them. Not only is that racist, but it's also child abuse.

Start being explicit about this. When the woke say something racist, get in their face and call them a racist. If they come back at you saying that you're the obvious racist, not them, stand your ground and point out explicitly why what they said was racist.

And it's not always just about race. The woke ideology is anti-human, anti-intellectual, anti-history, anti-reality, and anti-objectivity. It is oftentimes anti-Semitic, anti-capitalism, and downright un-American. Don't be afraid to say so.

## Troll Them Relentlessly

Listen, we've made it this far together, so let's be honest about something: Twitter is a hellscape of a website. It is the worst place on the internet. It brings out the darkest aspect of everyone who engages with it on a regular basis, including me.

And it is also the very best place to really piss off the woke. When you piss them off, they make mistakes. Oftentimes, they will say deeply incriminating things. When they do so, you can take advantage of them to make them look like the raging hypocrites that they are.

Trolling is defined by Urban Dictionary as a "deliberate act...of making random unsolicited and/or controversial comments on various internet forums with the intent to provoke an emotional knee jerk reaction."

In other words, your goal is to piss the woke off. It also happens to coincide with rule #4 for the actively unwoke: come at them, bro!

It's not that hard. Challenge their ideology in any way, and you'll likely provoke a reaction. Twitter isn't the only platform you can troll people on, but it truly is the best one for it because it is where most journalists get their news (a sad but true reality), and if you can get enough views on something, you could literally make headlines around the world. I've done it a few times with the Coke "Be Less White" training and outing anti-racist trainer Kate Slater for believing all white people are racist while being employed by a very white university.

The best part is that you can be totally anonymous on Twitter—you don't have to use your real name or photo. So, no excuses about potentially losing your job. Unless you're already banned on Twitter (which is a fair excuse), it's time to get your account up and running and get in the game. The worst thing that happens is that it will give you an outlet to blow off some steam on the woke. You can also support different unwoke activists while you're there by sharing their content.

Don't worry—it doesn't take very much effort to find woke people on Twitter. Just start by looking up almost any journalist at any major corporate press outfit or follow any of the people mentioned in this book as a good place to begin.

When you troll your woke targets, don't just call them names and hurl insults (and don't break Twitter's Terms of Service, because you'll just get your account banned, and that's no good for anyone). That's too easy, and strategically, it wins you no one. Instead, you want to be a little more artful about your trolling. Poke holes in their logic. Point out their hypocrisy. Provoke them into saying the quiet part out loud.

I once got an elected state representative to call me a racist on Twitter, simply because I supported the anti-CRT bill in New Hampshire. What did I do then? I turned around and quoted her calling me a racist in my testimony supporting the bill in front of her committee, proving the point emphatically (if albeit a little subversively) regarding why the bill was necessary in the first place. This is what Twitter is all about.

## Be Subversive

What if you printed off a bunch of bookmarks that said, "You are not a racist," brought them into your local woke independent bookstore, and gently placed them inside every anti-racist book they had on their bookshelf?

What if you logged into a public woke/anti-racist online training while it was happening live on the internet (they do these openly all the time) and said in the live chat, "Does this sound racist to anyone else?" Better yet, what if a team of you logged in and started asking different questions to poke holes in their material as if you're normal attendees?

What if you printed red bumper stickers with white lettering that said "Robin DiAngelo" and stuck them to stop signs throughout your neighborhood? (OK, you might want to check the legality on that one based on your local jurisdiction.)

Subversion is a good thing. And if you're really clever about it, you can get in people's heads in a way that logic and reason simply can't accomplish.

Generally speaking, I'm not a fan of the website 4chan—but I have to admit that they have some pretty epic wins with strategies just like this. For instance, they organized to hang up posters around communities that simply read, "It's OK to be white." Those posters started a firestorm, with many woke activists and media pundits declaring them divisive and racist.

Another 4chan troll is convincing the world that the "OK" hand signal (in which you bring your thumb and index finger together in a circle) is actually a white power hand gesture. They did this so they could find pictures of celebrities and politicians making the symbol (before it was considered racist) and call them a racist with photographic evidence.

And in the wake of George Floyd's death, they started a hashtag called #BaldforBLM which convinced women to completely shave their heads to stand against racism. Genius!

Have fun. Get creative. Make it a game to see who can come up with the best prank to expose how crazy these people really are.

## Clip Their Content

One day, just for fun, I created a two-minute clip of Robin DiAngelo saying she was a racist and that she believed all white people were racist, off a single training video posted by a public library in Seattle, Washington, on YouTube. The video went viral and was even featured on an episode of Dave Rubin's show *The Rubin Report*.

The woke *love* to put their materials online. There are entire social media accounts on places like YouTube and Instagram dedicated to helping people to become better anti-racist allies. The content is all right there for the taking; we just have to go and find it.

Want an example of what I'm talking about? Follow the Twitter account for Mythinformed (@MythinformedMKE). These guys put on a great conference called the Better Discourse Conference and post clips from these woke trainings all the time that expose these people for who they truly are, putting millions of eyes on their objectively insane points of view.

Here are some of the clips they've found:

- Robin DiAngelo saying that comedy is an excuse to be racist, and that it's OK to make fun of white people but not black people.
- A professor at Penn State telling a white student that they are being an oppressor by breathing. The same professor held a struggle session in his class for the sake of attempting to prove that Asian men are not seen as desirable sexual partners (that's racist!).
- A presenter at a Howard University conference saying the quiet part out loud when she acknowledged that the main goal of Critical Race Theory was to create a new system by acting as though the new system is already in place.
- A Drake University professor talking about their conversation with a child, telling them that Europeans have (for the most part) never done anything good and that white children must take responsibility for their ancestors.

This is all gold. And it's all on the internet because the guys behind Mythinformed took the time to suffer through the content and make the clips. Literally anyone with a laptop can do the same thing.

## Start a Book Club

*Animal Farm. 1984. Brave New World. Fahrenheit 451. Atlas Shrugged. The Fountainhead. V for Vendetta.* (Yes, it was a graphic novel before it was a movie.) When was the last time you read any of the classics? If you haven't recently, I strongly recommend you do because their relevance to our world today is absolutely frightening.

Frightening in a necessary, red pill kind of way.

What if you formed a book club in your neighborhood, just for fun, and you picked some of these titles to read and discuss? Maybe you invite some Democrats or people who haven't taken the red pill just yet, focusing on the content of the book as a classic work of literature, tricking them into reading it and inviting them into an open, totally non-political discussion on the implications. What a wonderful opportunity to discuss the similarities between the book and what we're experiencing now to help people wake up and see the world as it truly is!

You can form a book club with like-minded folks as well, of course. But why not try your hand at red pilling a few people while you're at it? Maybe you plant some seeds that begin to bloom later on down the line.

## Make Art

One of the reasons that I just adore Jodi Shaw is not just that she was brave enough to speak out about what happened to her at Smith College. It's that she had the proverbial balls to perform a rap video about her experience as a middle-aged white lady. And it was phenomenal! Just look up "The Smith College Library Rap" on YouTube and you'll find it. You have to watch it. It's so good!

Jodi understands the power of art to influence hearts and minds. And she's not the only person to make art out of mocking woke culture.

- Comedian Ryan Long's video titles include "When Wokes and Racists Actually Agree On Everything," "When Your Mom Is A Feminist," and "The Church of Woke." He's received over sixty million views on his YouTube channel.
- Musician Tom MacDonald's songs include "Snowflakes," "Fake Woke," "Clown World," and "No Lives Matter." He's received six hundred million views on his YouTube channel.
- Benjamin Boyce created a twenty-something part documentary that is the best, most complete reporting of what happened at the famed Evergreen State College woke meltdown of 2017. Benjamin was a student there when it happened and so had unique access and perspective to share with the world.
- Conservative activist Ashley St. Clair published a children's book called *Elephants Are Not Birds* to combat the work of radical trans activists.
- The Daily Wire has started producing unwoke entertainment, including a feature-length movie called *Run Hide Fight* and signed Gina Carano to a movie deal after she was fired from *The Mandalorian* for unwoke social media posts.

Countless creatives are designing unwoke t-shirts and stickers, writing music, crafting clever memes, and creating art to fight back by presenting a different perspective. Time to get your creative juices flowing and see what you can create to inspire others.

Sharing your art with the world isn't always comfortable. And if you're creating art for the unwoke, you're in a more dangerous position than most. But isn't art supposed to be a bit dangerous? Great art makes us think. It can inspire us. Make us laugh. And sometimes, it can make us cry. And any of those emotions are fine, because if you've elicited any of those feelings in someone, you know you've done your job.

## Support Individual Agency

Perhaps the most subversive thing a person can do in a world moving ever more dangerously to collectivism is to help as many individuals as possible to find their individual greatness.

Most of you have seen Maslow's Hierarchy of Needs at some point in your life. It's a pyramid diagram with basic human needs on the bottom (like food, water, shelter, sleep, and security), psychological needs in the middle (like relationships, friends, and self-esteem), and self-actualization needs at the very top. The idea is that you cannot achieve the highest level of the human experience without making sure your basic needs, and then your psychological needs, are taken care of. One could say that the higher you are up on the pyramid, the more evolved you are as a human being.

When I discussed how there are creators and destroyers in the world earlier in the book, that's essentially a play on the idea of the locus of control. Our locus of control is where we get our power from. Individuals with an external locus of control get their power from things outside of themselves. This puts them at a disadvantage because they will always be dependent on what others do to them, for better or worse. On the other hand, individuals with an internal locus of control believe that they are plotting their own course based on their actions, not based on the whims of others.

James Lindsay said it best when he said the best antidote for the woke is responsibility and accountability.

- The more people who have an internal locus of control, the less power the woke will have.
- The more people who have a high degree of self-worth, the less power the woke will have.
- The more people who are creators (rather than destroyers), the less power the woke will have.
- The more people who give attention to their higher-level needs instead of their lower-level needs, the less power the woke will have.

All things go up when the brain is in a state of positivity and optimism.

When I started coaching people professionally, I learned that if you didn't take care of your own house, you would be a terrible coach for your clients and potentially do more harm than good. So, start with yourself first. Read Jordan Peterson's *12 Rules for Life*. Get things together. Maybe even get a life coach (an unwoke one, of course). Make sure your bases are covered and that you're feeling really good. It's OK to be a little bit selfish and take care of your own needs.

Once you're squared away, be like Harriet Tubman and go back for others. Don't make it about politics—make it about helping other people to discover and achieve their dreams. Mentor people who need it. Support others and be that positive cheerleader. See the potential in others that they may not dare to see in themselves. Perhaps even become an (unwoke) life coach, counselor, therapist, social worker, and the like.

Connect with people on a human level and help them see that they have so much more potential than they might think.

When we have power over ourselves, it is impossible for the woke to have any power over us.

# PART 3

## Maintain Your Sanity

# You've Been Canceled. Now What?

One of Saul Alinsky's Rules for Radicals is, "*The threat is usually more terrifying than the thing itself.*" So, I'd be remiss if I didn't address the thing most people are afraid of when it comes to fighting the woke: what it's like to get canceled and how you can survive it.

Yes, getting canceled sucks. But it doesn't suck as badly as you think it does, and it is an eminently survivable situation for the vast majority of people.

I'm one of the rare people who has had the pleasure of getting canceled by both the woke on the left *and* the right. I was canceled by the left for taking the red pill in one of the most public possible ways, and I've been canceled by the right for (ironically) pointing out that they were starting to act like the monsters they were fighting on the woke left after Donald Trump left office! As it turns out, both sides are equally offended (and react with similar responses) when someone with a perceived platform tells them how screwed up they are.

Word to the wise kids, stay as politically independent as possible, even if you join a party, lest you become tribalist pod people!

It's a funny thing. The left and the right approach cancelation in very distinct ways. When the left comes to cancel you, it's goal oriented: They go after your career and your finances. They hit you where it hurts to make it more difficult for you to lead a normal life because that's the thing that's most likely to make us bend the knee—financial survival.

But when the right cancels you, they make it personal. They dig through everything they can find from your past to assassinate your character and socially ostracize you.

Neither is good, but on a practical level cancelation from the left is scarier because it inhibits your ability to pay your bills. Cancelation by the right hurts more on a personal level but is easier to dig out of. Although it's inconvenient, it usually doesn't get in the way of you taking care of the necessities of life.

But regardless of which direction the cancelation is coming from, it's not a pleasant experience. You never want to anticipate being canceled because doing so could help you create a self-fulfilling prophecy and inadvertently make it happen! However, it is not a bad idea to be aware of some tools for surviving it, should the time occur.

## You Always Remember Your First Time

I'll never forget the feeling of knowing, emphatically, that I was going to be canceled. It wasn't long after my Trump rally article had gone viral, maybe a week or so. Tim Pool had just started his live *Timcast IRL* podcast, and Jack Murphy was his first guest. I was more or less still in shock at the aftermath from the bomb that article dropped on my life.

If you've never had the fortune (or misfortune?) of suddenly and unexpectedly going viral on the internet, I think it's difficult to understand what a bizarre experience the whole thing is. Thankfully, I had the benefit of my work being shared for mostly positive reasons, but the exposure you get is still so different from any normal experience.

I had never wanted to be a public person and was just completely unprepared for that level of spotlight. You go from doing the same things you do every day one minute to having literally millions of eyes on you out of nowhere. It comes at you like an unstoppable force and is a rush of energy like you have never felt before in your life. The first time I really realized the scale of it, I literally had a panic attack. At the time, I was on the rower in my Orangetheory class having a meltdown in front of twenty other people. It was great.

So, as all of this was happening to me, I sat down on my couch in an absolute daze and turned on Tim's show just to have something on the TV, but not even fully able to focus on what was being said. Jack happened to be talking about his book, *Democrat to Deplorable*, which seemed apropos of what was going on in my life, and I remember wondering if it was a fated experience that I happened to turn on that particular episode.

Jack started telling the story of when he had been canceled, getting wrongfully fired from a job for the crime of wrongthink. He never said where he had been fired from. However, as I listened to his story, I picked up enough details about the city this took place in and the type of work he did to know one thing for sure: Jack Murphy had been fired by one of my current training clients, one who had already promised me work for that year.

This was not a big-name organization that would be a household name, but it was a place I had done several corporate trainings for in my organizational psychology practice. They had a great team and were developing into a reliable client who would send consistent work. But, though I liked her very much, I knew the human resources director there was *very* woke. She was one of the well-meaning woke—one who (I believe) went along with it for good reasons, believing that in order to be a good person you had to be an anti-racist ally.

But she was woke nonetheless, followed me on Twitter, and was already well aware that I had committed the sin of attending a Trump rally and declaring that his supporters were not Nazis. I knew I was done for.

Sure enough, a month or two later when the COVID lockdowns started, I posted a meme about "kung flu" for a bit of levity and posted a video on my YouTube channel with my favorite "kung flu" memes. Singing to the song of "Kung Fu Fighting" but replacing "fu" with "flu" had recently been declared a racist act by the woke, and I knew I was pushing it, but the meme just made me laugh so hard that I couldn't help it! And I knew plenty of Asian people who agreed with me, and who was I to question them? In the early days of a worldwide pandemic, the very last thing we should lose, I thought, was our sense of humor.

It wasn't long after I posted the video that I got an email from the HR director at this organization telling me that I was being just a little too racist, and she couldn't possibly expose her vulnerable oppressed staff to me. However, if I wanted to talk it over and repent for my racism, she would be open to discussing it with me.

I told her thanks but no thanks. And that brings us to the most critical tip to help you survive a cancelation: do not give in, ever.

## Engage Rule #7: Never Bend the Knee

The Amish have the practice of shunning members of their church who have fallen out of favor for violating a church rule. It might include refusing to sit at the same table with the person to eat, even if they live in your own household, refusing to do business with the person, not accepting rides or gifts, and excluding them from community activities.

The purpose of shunning is to preserve the integrity of the church from a deviant member, to send a signal to other church members of what happens if you step out of line, and to elicit a change of heart in the individual who is breaking the rules. If the rule breaker comes around, they have to make a confession in front of the congregation and, at some point afterwards, all will be forgiven.

Here's the difference between being shunned by the Amish and canceled by the woke: The Amish provide a path to redemption—you make your grand confession, and you are welcomed back into the fold with the past forgotten. However, when you're canceled by the woke, there is no such path. They will make you believe that there is a path—that if you just say the right words then it will all be over. But it is not true. Saying you're sorry will never be enough. Once you do it, there will always be more asks, more demands, and your past transgressions will perpetually be used against you whenever it's convenient.

This is the most important thing you have to understand when the cancelation starts: the only way to come out of it with your integrity intact is to continue through it to the other side. No matter how bad it gets, no matter what they accuse you of, no matter how they smear you, you do not bend the knee *ever.*

The first mistake so many people make when they are being canceled is to assume that, because they have so many people after them, they have done something wrong. They look for a way to compromise and may even issue an apology for whatever transgression they are being attacked for. They will do anything they can think of just to make it stop.

In doing so, they overlook one key point: The woke mob doesn't want apologies. It doesn't want logic. It doesn't want reason. It ONLY wants vengeance. Once you give them an inch, they will take that mile. They will demand more and more, particularly if you commit any minor infraction that they might consider a microaggression in the future. They will just use it as an opportunity to make more demands and will always keep you at their mercy because they know you will give in.

This is a game of power, plain and simple. In order to survive it, you must show them that you are more powerful than they are. You must stand your ground, no matter how bad it gets. The minute you surrender is the minute you give them power over you.

I mentioned earlier that I had been canceled by both the right and the left. Well, my most recent cancelation (as of this writing, anyway!) came from the alt-right. Yes, the alt-right is a real thing. They don't make up the majority of the political right like the media tries to say they do. They are a tiny fraction of generally bad people among millions of good, kind conservatives, and their actions manage to give everyone else a bad name.

Nonetheless, they are very real. I found that out when I refused to use the term "anti-white" to describe Critical Race Theory.

In the spring and summer of 2021, the fight against Critical Race Theory began to attract a lot of national attention as several states introduced legislation to ban it on a state level. I had been working on bringing attention to a bill in my home state of New Hampshire by traveling throughout the state and meeting with different groups to help people understand what CRT was and why it was bad, because it was still a very new concept for many. My goal was to support efforts to legislate against taxpayer dollars funding more divisive concepts from being taught as fact. If people knew what was being taught, they tended to support the bill banning it.

In May, I began to notice people I was speaking with referring to CRT as "anti-white" at many of the in-person meetings I was attending. I understood it—on its surface, if you don't understand that it's racist against every skin color, it can seem like it's entirely made up of anti-white components. Those components are the ones that are typically shown on conservative newscasts on the subject. Even I'm guilty of being the person who broke the story of Coke's "Be Less White" training. It made sense that people who were just learning about the topic would describe it in terms of simplicity.

But it's important to understand that Critical Race Theory is not just anti-white. It is racist against every skin color but for different reasons. No form of racism is any better or worse than any other form of racism, and our goal should be to achieve a color-indifferent society based on individualism and meritocracy. Focusing just on the anti-white impact, to me, is just as bad as saying black lives matter—it is two sides of the same coin and doesn't get us any further to the goal. I was completely, totally against it and believed that using that language would only lead to more racism, not less.

Not long after I noticed this "anti-white" language showing up in person, I began to notice it online. Now, oftentimes trends will show themselves online before they show up in person. That's why I paid particular attention to the "anti-white" language—I noticed the trend in person before I noticed it online. Another thing I learned from seeing it show up in person is that the people using it would get *very* agitated when I tried to explain that CRT wasn't just anti-white, it was anti-everyone. Their reaction was completely out of proportion to the point where they would end up having completely counterproductive conversations.

I did more and more digging regarding this language because I could see it become an unhelpful attribute of the legitimate fight against Critical Race Theory. Frankly, if you have a bunch of people on the political right complaining about how something is "anti-white," that is going to look very racist and will only serve as confirmation for every terrible accusation the progressive left makes about them. That gives the left more power to make more demands. Our goal is to make sure they get less power, not more.

What I found was both shocking and not at all surprising at the same time. The "anti-white" language to describe Critical Race Theory was coming from groups advancing ideas around "white wellbeing," "white positivity," and even "white survival." There was a not-insignificant group of people who truly believed that there was going to be a holocaust against white people at any moment. It was one of the scariest descents into madness that I have ever experienced, but it wasn't a surprising one. I had long been afraid of a reality in which a legitimate white power movement started to make a comeback in response to Critical Race Theory and the woke left.

Well, here we are. And to make matters worse, it's supported by some very popular conservative influencers who care more about attention than they do about standing up for what is right.

When I say a "white power" movement, I don't mean it in the way that the woke left would refer to someone as a white supremacist or racist. I mean an actual white power movement—people who are placing priority on those with white skin above others. The whole idea isn't in opposition to Critical Race Theory—it directly supports it! Critical Race Theory straight up says that white people are at the top of the food chain. These people are more than happy to agree!

To make a long story short, I declared that I would not refer to Critical Race Theory as "anti-white" on the internet and implored people to exercise responsibility and do the same. Just because you can say something doesn't mean you should say something, and given what I had learned, I viewed the language as detrimental to our larger goal.

That's when something I never expected happened: legitimate white identitarians began mobbing me, brigading my YouTube channel, writing smear pieces about me, digging up old photos of me posing with Democratic politicians as though it were a major revelation that I had been a Democrat, and more. They attacked my supporters who spoke up in my favor.

The memes of me photoshopped as a pig were particularly delightful.

And to make it even better, individuals on the right who were outside looking in at this happening, some of whom I had always defended, made it their business to sharpen their knife and stab me in the back repeatedly to take advantage of what was going on. This was one of the most painful, heart-breaking, disappointing things that has happened to me on my journey—the absolute and utter betrayal of being left hanging completely out to dry was indescribably lonely. There were a few exceptions of individuals who had my back, but mostly it showed the true colors of many that I had trusted, some of whom I had called friends.

The worst of it lasted for almost three weeks, though I experienced ramifications of it for far longer. All because I refused to say that Critical Race Theory is "anti-white."

But I didn't bend the knee. I didn't relent. And, to this day, I refuse to use any terminology that places the impact of woke culture more on one race than on any other race. Our goal is a color-indifferent world. We can't achieve that without being indifferent towards color. Racism is wrong, period.

Any cancelation is a test of the courage of your convictions—how much are you willing to sacrifice to be able to look yourself in the mirror every day and know you stood for something?

## Pain Is Temporary

The thing that got me through that particular cancelation was the knowledge that, at some point, it would be over. At some point, people would move on to the next outrage, I would have all the worst perpetrators blocked so that I wouldn't have to hear from them anymore, and I could refocus on what I was supposed to be working on: helping individuals empower themselves to fight back against the woke in their lives. As long as you stand your ground and take away their ability to have that power over you, they always move on eventually.

When I use the term "cancelation," I use it very loosely to refer to an angry mob of people coming for you in some way. Maybe they aren't trying to get you fired from your job or destroy your life, but that's not what it feels like when it's happening. Minimally, they make your life very difficult with the pure intent of pressuring you to do what they want you to do.

Most "cancelations" last a day or two and usually involve more inconvenience than cancelation—lots of mean tweets, angry messages, and so on. Usually, it's mostly harmless, but make sure you report any threats of violence to the police so that they know what's going on. Document everything you can because you don't know when you might need it.

Some cancelations last longer, and some have long-term consequences, like the loss of a job or (worst case scenario) your name becoming publicly synonymous with the cancelation. One example of that is famed trans-racial activist Rachel Dolezal. These cancelations are absolutely more difficult situations to deal with, but they are not insurmountable. As time goes on, the vast majority of people who go through it are able to get things back on track, and you have to trust that you can do the same. Many even use their cancelation to thrive.

The reality is that there are so many people and things being canceled at any given time these days that chances are most cancelations are on the more minor side unless it's a *really* crazy story. Even very high-profile things are usually forgotten in a week and, after you have a little time to recover, you'll be telling the story of your cancelation at cocktail parties saying the whole experience made you stronger.

No matter how bad it gets, you will get through it as long as you don't give up. You will feel much better on the other side if you are true to yourself and what you believe, rather than selling out under the false belief that it will make things easier.

## Disconnect and Reflect

We can always look at things that happen to us as negative or positive. Yes, I know that's hard when it seems like the world is trying to rip your life apart, but this is a moment that can also allow you to reflect and strengthen the convictions you hold dear.

To do this, you've got to disconnect. Get off the internet. Just turn it off. Stop looking at the responses, the messages, the videos, the news, or anything else. Trust me, they're not going to stop anyway, and you will gain nothing by continuing to give them any part of your attention.

Instead, go out in the real world and talk to normal people. Call up your best friend. Maybe even find a therapist or coach to connect with (a non-woke one of course!). Focus on people you can have deep conversations with. Look at the bigger picture. If you're a religious or spiritual person, now is a perfect time to connect with God in whatever way works best for you.

The internet, the media—it's all nonsense. Truly. It's just a circus, filled with people pretending to do the news but who are really just selling us ideological entertainment on both sides of the spectrum. Most influencers are completely corrupt, talking heads at best (yes, even the ones you probably like). And when you step back and look at how amazing and beautiful life can be when you just tune it all out, that's when all of this can come back into perspective.

Cancelation is meant to put you under stress. There is no other point but to cause you pain until you break. But you can mitigate a lot of that stress by simply choosing not to engage with it and taking the time to take care of yourself instead.

With a new perspective and a quieted mind, take a moment to ask yourself a simple question: Did you stand up for what was right?

That's the crux of it, isn't it? Did you stand up for what was right, or didn't you? Not what was convenient. Not what would be the easiest. Not what would be more accepted in polite company—did you stand up for what was *right*?

In *12 Rules for Life*, Jordan Peterson says, "If you betray yourself, if you say untrue things, if you act out a lie, you weaken your character."

Cancelation is a test of staying true to what is fair, just, and correct, and knowing what you truly value when your back is slammed against a wall. And if you didn't do anything wrong, then you have absolutely nothing to feel ashamed for. The mob does not get to decide what's right, no matter how much they demand to anoint themselves.

Expression is not only guaranteed to us by the First Amendment in this country, but it's also a gift given to us by God simply because we exist. You don't have to do anything to earn the right to express yourself—you have it because you are here. And many people forget that free speech is only protected for all of us when we defend the speech that some find indefensible. Unpopular speech is the only speech that requires protection.

No matter what your speech was, you almost certainly had the right to say it. And if you stood up for what is fair and just in the process, all the better.

## Make Yourself Uncancelable

A lot of you reading this may have found me through my YouTube channel, but the truth is being on video and having public attention isn't my favorite thing to do. There are times I want to quit more than I can say (cancelation sucks after all!), but the reason I keep doing it is precisely because it provides me with a steady stream of income. And that income gives me the freedom to speak up and write books like this. You don't need absolute financial security to truly embrace expression… but man, does it make it easier.

Thomas Jefferson famously quipped that he would prefer dangerous freedom to peaceful slavery. The only way to make yourself truly uncancelable is to embrace the dangerous freedom of entrepreneurship. Embrace capitalism. Make your own money. Figure out ways to rely on as few people as possible for your income.

Entrepreneurship can be terrifying, but the reality is that it can also be liberating. When I was canceled the first time, I was already running my own business and so I had a bit of a leg up. I knew I could always create new product lines or trainings to be able to replace anything that was lost.

My first cancelation made a few things very clear:

1. I had to create multiple sources of income if I wanted to continue to speak out publicly. Relying on one or two

sources of income wouldn't be enough to suffice—I had to create multiple redundancies to be truly safe.

2. I couldn't take on any long-term consulting work while I was speaking publicly—I had to focus on offerings that were easier and quicker to deliver before anyone noticed I was that anti-CRT woman and could have me canceled for it.
3. I had to make sure that all of my contracts and service agreements had very strict cancelation policies just in case I was canceled close to launch or midway through a project. This worked out beautifully when I was canceled after just one week of a four-week training program. (The crime I committed to earn the cancelation was getting retweeted by Donald Trump when he still had a Twitter account.) Even though I only completed 25 percent of the project, I got 100 percent of the fee. Winning!

So, I reformatted my business. I made changes to my offerings. I added new things on. Some things succeeded and others failed, but I didn't let the failures stop me from moving forward.

Now, not all of you will be in a place where you can start a full-time business, and I understand that. But what you can do is start a side hustle. That was how I built my own business—I was working a full-time job in Boston (an hour or ninety-minute commute by bus from my house each way, depending on traffic), and I spent all of my time on my commute building my side hustle. It took years of work. It didn't happen overnight. But slowly it did. Five years after I started it, I made the leap to do it full-time. I was scared. There were months I didn't know how I would pay the bills. But it always worked out. The day I decided to do it, I told myself that everyone who had ever done this in their life had been scared. That meant I was in exactly the place I should have been.

By the way, in my first book, *Zen Your Work*, I wrote a whole chapter about how to discover your true passions in your career and about how you can make a living doing almost anything.

So, start thinking of ways you can make money. There are millions of ways to do it—don't put any limitations on yourself. If you could do anything, what would you do? Brainstorm first, and then figure out a way to make it workable. If you can dream it, you can do it. It's just that some dreams require more time/energy than others.

And once you've made it (maybe you already have), then it's especially important for us self-employed people to go the extra mile to do what's right—oftentimes, we are in a better position to stick up for the things worth fighting for than people who might face more severe consequences, like losing a job.

## You Have More People on Your Side Than You Think

I thank God every day for my Locals community (https://kb.locals.com!). Locals, created by Dave Rubin specially to battle cancel culture and big tech censorship, is a community-based platform that has safeguards in place to make it literally the only sane place on the internet. There are no trolls, no hecklers—just real people who want to connect based on shared interests. And it's in my Locals community that I'm constantly reminded of how much support I have, even when things get really bad externally. If I've done my job right, I'm not the only one who finds support in the community—I hope my members also find support when they need it most. When you're fighting back against the woke, community is so important because it's a consistent reminder that you will always have more people who love you than hate you.

When you're in the midst of a cancelation, it can truly seem as though the entire world is against you. Looks can be deceiving. The loudest people are always the ones who hold the most anger and, sadly, the ones you have in your corner rarely speak up. It's not that they don't want to. It's just that a lot of times they don't know what to say or do to help, and they're afraid of being attacked themselves. Try not to judge them too harshly when it's all over.

It's important to find the people who love you. The people you can trust. The people who will hold your hand through thick and thin and keep telling you that it's going to be OK. These are the people who will still be there after the mob has moved on to their next target. Even though it can be natural to focus on the negative—that's part of our survival mechanism—try instead to intentionally focus as much of your energy and attention on the right people, not the ones making all of the noise. Every time you feel your attention drift away, bring it back to where it rightfully belongs. Do everything you can to make it feel as though the people who love you are the majority. That will make the people who don't care about you feel like an afterthought.

## Is Cancelation Inevitable?

Is cancelation more likely to happen when you're fighting the woke? Sure!

Is it an inevitability? No. And you should never treat it like it is because human beings have a great way of creating self-fulfilling prophecies. When you worry about something often, you are more likely to behave in a way that will actually cause that thing to happen. Thus, you create the thing you are most afraid of!

You cannot control if you are canceled. You can only control how you handle it. So, stop worrying so much and, if it happens, you can deal with it at that point. If you've followed the previous advice in this book, you have all the tools available at your disposal to survive your cancelation and come out swinging on the other side.

"*The threat is usually more terrifying than the thing itself.*" When you give into the fear of cancelation, you're doing exactly what the woke wants you to do.

Instead, play by your own rules: "*Even if the thing happens, I have nothing to fear.*"

# Self-Care for the Unwoke

Let's be honest: fighting the woke can be exhausting, frustrating, confounding, and downright infuriating. You see the worst in human beings, and it can very well break your spirit if you let it.

Several times in this book, we've come back to the idea that this is a battle of attrition: it will only end when one side gives up. That means the goal is not so much to win a decisive, earth-shattering victory—it's simply to exhaust the other side until they surrender and leave the battlefield.

That means a critical part of the process must be self-care. We not only have to make it more painful for the woke to stay on the battlefield than to leave, we also have to make sure we don't quit until that happens. Our goal is nothing short of getting every last woke ally out of any position of decision-making power. We don't do this by cancelation like the woke. Instead, our job is to wake as many people up to their plans as we possibly can and change culture. And, because that's a long-term proposition, we simultaneously need to throw sand in their gears in the meantime.

That means we have to take care of our energy and our perspective. Lucky thing is, my first book was all about mindfulness in the workplace, and so I know lots of strategies for reducing stress and maintaining your perspective in less-than-ideal situations. Let's dig in.

## Your Emotions Dictate Your Experience

I know, I know—some of you reading this may not want to talk about squishy things like feelings, particularly when they are fighting an enemy that is almost entirely driven by their negative emotions. But in order to take care of ourselves, we simply must address feelings because the emotions we have at any given moment will dictate whether or not we have a positive experience in the world. The more positive our experiences, the more likely we are to stay the course.

Remember that locus of control thing we talked about a few chapters ago? Oftentimes, people believe that the emotions we experience are the result of things that happen to us. If something negative happens to us, we experience negative emotions as a result of the thing that happened. If something positive happens to us, we experience positive emotions as a result of the thing that happened, and so on, and so forth.

The problem is that it's completely untrue, as evidenced by the simple fact that we all know people who always seem to be in a good mood no matter what happens. The difference between the people who live a mostly happy life and those who live a mostly unhappy life is that those who live a mostly happy life simply make the choice to be happy, no matter what. They don't sweat the small stuff. They don't allow anyone to make them feel less than worthy. They understand how to focus their energy and attention on creating a positive perspective and experience, even in less-than-ideal circumstances.

Here's a simple exercise to make this feel more real: Close your eyes for a moment (after you finish reading about the exercise of course) and take in three to five long, deep breaths. Once you're relaxed, think about a time in your life when you were truly happy. Allow it to be the first thing that pops into your mind, because that's usually the best answer. Feel the emotions of happiness, joy, contentment, bliss, optimism, and the like wash over you and relive whatever memory gave them to you in the first place. Allow yourself to smile, maybe even giggle or laugh at the memory as you live it as though it were currently happening in your mind's eye. Stay in that memory for as long as you can and let yourself feel at peace.

When you feel at peace, open your eyes. How do you feel?

If you did the exercise and are being honest with yourself, you probably feel great. If you do, congratulations. You just made the choice to experience a specific emotion out of nowhere, based on nothing more than a memory. You may even feel like you can take on the world! Good. That's exactly where we need you.

The emotions we experience in our heads not only impact how we behave in situations but also how others respond to us. Remember, one of the things we need to accomplish (rule #11) is waking up more people on the left, and that means we have to create a safe environment for them to land where they feel comfortable putting themselves in a vulnerable position.

Choosing the right emotions when we're engaged in battle is going to be critical. Not only will it help you, it will also help them. And, as you just experienced, we can always make the choice to experience a different emotion if we want to see the world differently from our current perspective.

Let me give you an example from my longtime coach Joshua MacGuire (better known as Joshua the Psychic on my YouTube channel). Joshua has been in charge of helping me to maintain my perspective for years. Don't be fooled by the psychic stuff, if that's not your thing. Joshua is a very experienced coach and someone who is responsible for many of the successes I've been able to muster on this journey. The reason he is successful is because he lives his own strategies.

Joshua places a very high premium on his happiness and is committed to doing what is required to maintain a high emotional state. He's also a creature of habit, which means that he has a very stable routine that he is committed to every day. Part of that routine is that he goes to Starbucks each morning and gets his coffee like clockwork.

One morning, Joshua walked in and there was a new barista behind the counter. Wouldn't you know it, but she gave him the stink eye! This kept happening day after day. Joshua would walk in as his happy, perky self, and his mood would be thrown off by the stink eye. He knew something had to be done.

Joshua is experienced enough to know that he couldn't change the barista, he could only change how he was approaching and interacting with the barista. So, he employed this strategy to get his mood back on track:

> *It's not about what I think of myself. I think I'm pretty great.*

*It's not what she thinks of me. I can't control that because I can only control myself.*

*It's what* I think *she thinks of me. That's the element I need to change.*

The main problem that Joshua was experiencing in this situation was that his head was telling him that the barista was giving him the stink eye because she didn't like him. The idea of someone not liking him was impacting his mood. And his commitment to a positive experience dictated that he disrupt the entire situation.

So, he simply made the choice to change what he believed the barista thought of him. It's a head game—how we perceive the situation will dictate how we manage our energy in it and how we direct our attention.

The next day, instead of walking into the Starbucks with the perspective that this barista hated him, he sauntered in with ease, confidently telling himself, "She totally wants me." How do you act when you know someone has a crush on you? You feel good about yourself. You have an extra swagger. Maybe you flirt a little.

And that's exactly what he did. Every day, he sauntered in, flirted with her, completely committed to the idea that she wasn't giving him the stink eye because she hated him. She was doing it because she had a crush on him and was dealing with it like kids on the playground do!

Of course, at first, she looked at him like he had three heads. But after he committed to the perspective and behaved as if it were the complete and total truth every day, she started to soften up. Not long after, she was giving him free coffee in the morning!

By going in with a positive mental headspace, Joshua was able to achieve a better outcome for himself. But more importantly, he allowed himself to live an experience that felt good even before he achieved the desired end result.

The war with the woke will be a long one. It will not be settled in a year or two—it will be going on for decades. We need to be able to feel great even when we may be a long way off from achieving our goals.

Practice committing to an emotion first and then take action to support the emotion you've chosen. Without even realizing it, you'll create a more positive experience. And you'll make it more comfortable for people to change their attitudes and behaviors as well, which will lead to more people waking up.

## Do Things You Love

I'm writing this chapter after returning from a weekend where I got to do one of my favorite things: spend four days buying art. I started collecting when I was in college, mostly concert posters that I thought were cool. eBay was my place of choice to buy. Then, when I was traveling a lot for work, I would always spend time in new cities visiting local galleries as something to do. Eventually, I graduated to fine art when I was blessed enough to have the means to do it.

You always remember the first artist who took your breath away. For me, it was David Najar, an Israeli artist who paints the most stunning landscapes. They look like something out of a dream. After Najar, it was Ashton Howard. After Howard, it was Kre8 and his protégé Sneak. The more I fought the woke, the more of their art I bought to surround myself with, because I genuinely love it. It brings me joy and helps me to balance out all of the nonsense.

Life is about balance. If you spend all day reading bad news, of course, you're going to think the world is a terrible place! One of the things that can help you maintain your chosen emotions so much easier is to commit to experiencing just as much positive in life as you do negative. That's why it's so important to give yourself the gift of time doing things that feed your energy to balance the time you spend depleting your resources by doing battle with woke.

- What do you love to do?
- What could you do for hours without stopping to look at the clock?
- What makes you feel amazing?

Be honest with yourself about your answers to these questions. I didn't ask you what would make you money or what would make your family happy—I asked you what you LOVE. What you love is something that is just for you, no matter how anyone else feels about it.

Once you know what your thing is, make time to do that or be around it. Maybe your passion is travel. Well, we can't spend our time perpetually on vacation, but we can watch videos about traveling to different destinations around the world. You may not be able to buy expensive art, but you can go to museums and galleries to enjoy it. Maybe you aren't destined to be a world-famous rock star, but you can still grab your guitar and enjoy every second of making music.

A car can't drive forever without stopping to fuel up occasionally. Human beings need to fuel up as well. You're not being selfish by taking care of yourself—you're making sure you have the fuel you need to make it to the end of a long journey.

## Support Each Other

We've discussed the power of support groups in different places in this book, but usually in the context of a tool to rally support for fighting the woke. But sometimes you just need people to talk to who understand.

I have a weekly support group of whistleblowers and dissidents who all understand what it's like to fight back against the woke and how much of a toll it can take on your experience. There's no pressure, no expectation—we just show up to our Zoom call from wherever we are in the world to talk and support one another. We laugh. We brainstorm. We provide a kinder perspective than all the noise we might hear on social media. We trust one another. And in between our weekly chats, we can rely on each other if it really hits the fan.

You can do the same thing with any of the support groups you've created to help you fight back. Don't just go to war together, be at peace together too. It's OK to allow people to support you.

If you're struggling to find other people like you, join my Locals community, and we'll hook you up with positivity and support. There are other wonderful groups out there you can connect with on Locals and other platforms that will help you maintain your sanity. I like Locals the best because their model really keeps out the trolls and outrage so you can find yourself around normal people attempting to have authentic human interactions.

## Allow Yourself to Laugh

There are so many hilarious things that are going on right now:

- Trump issuing press releases as a way of avoiding his permanent Twitter ban because he knows people will take a photo and tweet them.
- Really awful woke progressives posting incriminating videos of themselves on TikTok.
- James Lindsay's daily feed on Twitter (assuming he hasn't been suspended by the time you're reading this).

Even as the world burns, it's important to make sure you allow yourself to enjoy the simple pleasures these gifts offer. And they are gifts—laughing lowers our stress levels, making us better fighters when we get back to business.

When Trump was elected in 2016, I wasn't happy about it. But I also managed the situation a lot better than most of my lefty friends because I found humor in it. Even as I was watching MSNBC nightly, convinced that collusion with Russia was a real thing, I still laughed. And I truly believe that's one of the things that kept me from getting sucked into the woke mindset—I genuinely found the entire thing hilarious.

Yes, the things that the woke are doing to our society are serious, but it's OK to have a sense of humor about it. If something is funny, don't feel bad to laugh about it, enjoy it, and share it with your friends! Humor is always preferable over anger—if you don't laugh, you'll probably end up crying.

## Meditate

Yeah, OK. I know meditation seems woo-woo and cheesy for some of you, but it truly is the magic bullet when it comes to mental health.

Meditation is a gift that you give yourself to spend a few moments every day focused entirely on you. It keeps you grounded, can build your confidence, help you create visions for successful realities, and teaches you how to focus your energy and attention on the things that matter the most.

There is no right way to meditate. You can do it sitting, standing, or even walking. You can do it in the day or night. You can meditate for five minutes or five hours. You can listen to guided meditations to have something to focus your energy on, or you can just shut your eyes, breathe deeply, and let yourself go.

The best way to know what works for you is to experiment and try out a lot of different types of meditation. Look for apps or free guided meditations on YouTube or Spotify just to get started.

When you first start, it will be hard, but accept that. Create a small, achievable goal and just shoot for five minutes a day of meditation. Once you can do that well, try ten minutes. The important thing is not the length—it's the consistency. Show up determined to give yourself that precious gift every single day for thirty days. At the end, evaluate how you feel and where you'll take your practice from there.

I've yet to meet a single person who regretted learning to meditate—there's a reason for it. It's a game changer, but you must have faith that you must go through the part where meditation is hard to discover the place where meditation is easy, valuable, and incredibly fulfilling.

## Be Grateful

No matter what happens in life, whether you had a good day or a bad day, one of the very best things you can do is focus your attention on the positive by grounding your day in gratitude.

The sun is shining, making it a great day for a walk.

You've got a roof over your head, giving you shelter.

Your bills are paid, giving you security.

You had a great sandwich for lunch that left you totally satisfied.

You got followed by your favorite influencer, making you feel excited.

You just completed knitting an amazing shawl that you'll love wearing.

No matter what is going on, you can always ground your day in gratitude.

A few years back, researchers from the Hong Kong Institute of Education conducted a rather simple experiment. They recruited one hundred healthcare professionals (made up of physicians, nurses, physiotherapists, and occupational therapists) and split them into three groups to explore the possible benefits of gratitude.

- *Gratitude*: The first group was instructed to keep a journal of work-related events in which they expressed gratitude or thanks for something they appreciated about their day, such as a colleague swapping schedules with them or helping them out in a way that made their job easier. This was the group with the "gratitude" condition.

- *Hassle*: The second group was instructed to keep a similar journal with one crucial distinction: instead of focusing on things they were grateful for, this group was instructed to write about the things that hassled them at work, such as having an exhausting day or being annoyed at a comment from a patient's relative. This group was assigned the "hassle" condition.
- *Control*: The third group was the control group and did not participate in keeping a journal so to create a baseline by which to judge the other two interventions.

The experiment lasted just one month, with both the gratitude group and the hassle group writing an experience in their journal twice a week. At the end of the month, the results were clear: those who journaled about experiences they were grateful for showed a significant decline in both stress and depressive symptoms, while the other two groups showed no noticeable change.

Practicing gratitude is the mindful act of focusing your energy and attention on the things that enhance the human experience, rather than focusing on the things that detract from it. And when you're fighting the woke, you will experience more than your fair share of things that detract from the human experience! If you find yourself focusing on them, don't be too hard on yourself—that's part of our natural survival mechanism.

When you become consciously aware of what you're doing, just gently nudge yourself back in the other direction by making a list of the positive aspects of your experience. It doesn't need to be a big, earth-shattering thing for you to be grateful for it.

Robert Emmons, one of the world's leading scientific experts on gratitude, notes there are two elements to consider in your practice. The first is the affirmation of goodness, or the acknowledgement of the gifts and benefits you've received. The second is the understanding that the source of the gifts is outside of ourselves. It could be your friend, colleagues, boss, family, or even a higher power.

At the end of a long day, make a quick list of the things you're grateful for. It will serve as a consistent reminder that the world is so much more amazing than the woke would have us believe. And that's something worth fighting for.

# Fight Like James Lindsay

I've mentioned James Lindsay several times throughout this book. And that's because he is the absolute role model I follow when it comes to fighting back effectively against the woke ideology. He the woke's greatest nightmare—someone who truly understands what they are doing, is able to clearly articulate it to others, and who takes exactly zero grief when they come for him. And he just keeps going.

James Lindsay is one of the authors of the *Grievance Studies*, a series of fake academic papers that were published in woke journals to prove how low the academic peer review standards really are.

He is the founder of New Discourses, the most comprehensive site on the internet explaining the woke ideology for the masses.

He has studied the woke intimately, read their academic writings, understands what they believe, how they developed, and what they are trying to do better than anyone on the planet.

He has the most based Twitter account on the planet, where he demonstrates his mastery of the artful troll every day of the week.

He is authentic and absolutely unapologetic in his approach.

And he has a giant sword.

That's why the last thought I want to leave you with before you graduate and join the unwoke army is this: *fight like James Lindsay.*

Fight as if you understand completely that this is a battle for the soul of our country. It is not a time to pussyfoot around or waste time on nonsense. We have work to do.

Stop being afraid of what other people think, if you'll be called a nasty name, or if you'll get mean tweets. None of that matters in the long run, and you're strong enough to survive all of it and more.

Don't worry that you might lose people in your life. Yes, it sucks, but for every door that closes, another will open. Not all relationships are meant to last forever, and the people who truly love you won't be scared off that easily.

Continue to learn as much as you can. This book was meant to be a good general overview of the elements we're fighting, written for everyone who might just be getting introduced to the topic. Volumes could be written, and we would still only scratch the surface of the woke. You've got a good foundation, but never stop learning as long as you're in the fight, because the better you know your enemy, the more likely you are to be able to defeat them.

Be smart about the battles you're choosing to fight. Put your energy where it can do the most good and use your unique talents to your advantage.

Be brave. Act authentically. Have courage. Every time you express yourself you can inspire others to do the same.

And no matter what happens, enjoy life. Never ever let the woke take that joy away from you. Nothing will piss them off more than if you just smile at them before walking away to do exactly what you want to do.

When you join the unwoke army, you won't be by yourself. I know it may seem like it, but I promise that if you make the most minimal effort to connect with other people in this fight, you will find friends and allies. You'll find people who see the world the way you do, who know what's happening is wrong, and who are willing to stand up for what is right.

This book has given you everything you need to get started. It's provided more direction than most people had when they got into this fight. You have to trust that you're ready to join the battle. And if you believe in the experiment that was started in 1776 (not 1619), you have a responsibility to do it.

We don't fight this battle because it is convenient. We fight this battle because it is necessary and because we know that no one is coming to save us.

We may not be able to win. We may not be able to beat back the cultural revolution that has already started. But given the choice between rolling over and accepting defeat or standing up for what I believe in to the bitter end, I will choose the latter every single time.

Always remember that the numbers are on our side. We just have to wake them up, inspire them to action by making the case for why our way is better, and provide a role model for them to follow.

What happens if every single person reading this book inspires just one person to become actively unwoke? And then all of those people inspire one more person, and so on and so forth, with each person fighting back in their own unique way?

If we can do it, we'll be unstoppable. And it's not an unreasonable aspiration.

So, we know what success looks like, and we know how to get there. Now, let's go win the war and create our color-indifferent society grounded in individualism and meritocracy, where everyone has equal access to opportunities regardless of how they were born.

Our enemies have been doing this for a while, but we'll do it better. And we'll outlast anything they can throw at us.

Let's go.

# Acknowledgments

I would not be here today without my husband, Victor, who has held my hand, heard me cry, comforted me when I was canceled or when I wanted to give up, and been a constant source of love and support. I would be lost without him. Victor, I love you more than words can say.

My coach and friend, Joshua MacGuire, has been with me every step of the way. Writing this book took a lot out of me, and Joshua was always there to provide me with unconditional support. I can't give you enough credit for what you've done for me in this lifetime, Joshua.

Thank you to James Lindsay, Chris Rufo, and Corey DeAngelis who showed me what it means to be a warrior and to never give up. To Dave Rubin, for being a role model for all of us in what it means to be brave and change your mind. To Brandon Straka, for showing me what it means to fight for what you believe in, and to the entire #WalkAway family for being a safe place for people to land on their red pill journey. To the knitting community, for being a bunch of badass women (and a few men) who weren't afraid to stand up and fight back. To the LPNH, the Free State Project, and the Mises Caucus where I found my political home and have given me faith that we can win in the long run. And to everyone whose story I told in the book who has taken action in the face of adversity to stand up for what is right. I hope your stories inspire thousands more just like you.

Finally, of course, thank you to the community on Locals, YouTube, Twitter, and whatever social network you've found me on. You have no idea how many times I relied on you to lift me up, and many of you have stepped up in ways I could never have dreamed. You are too many to list, and I wouldn't want to make the mistake of leaving out anyone who was deserving. Just know that I appreciate you and love you all. You are proof that life is awesome, that average people can make a difference, and that we can win this fight if we all come together.